COMMON CORE ACHIEVE

Mastering Essential Test Readiness Skills

HiSET® Exercise Book

SOCIAL STUDIES

Mc Graw Hill Education

Bothell, WA • Chicago, IL • Columbus, OH • New York, NY

MHEonline.com

Send all inquiries to:
McGraw-Hill Education
8787 Orion Place
Columbus, OH 43240

ISBN: 978-0-02-143265-3
MHID: 0-02-143265-1

Printed in the United States of America.

3 4 5 6 7 8 9 RHR 19 18 17 16 15 14

Table of Contents

Congratulations! If you are using this book, it means that you are taking a key step toward achieving an important new goal for yourself. You are preparing to take the *HiSET*® exam in order to earn your high school diploma, one of the most important steps in the pathway toward career, educational, and lifelong well-being and success.

Common Core Achieve: Mastering Essential Test Readiness Skills is designed to help you learn or strengthen the skills you will need when you take the *HiSET*® exam. The Social Studies Exercise Book provides you with additional practice of the key concepts and skills required for success on test day and beyond.

How to Use This Book

This book is designed to follow the same lesson structure as the Core Student Module. Each lesson in the Social Studies Exercise Book is broken down into the same sections covering key concepts as the core module, with a page or more devoted to the topics covered in each section. Each lesson contains at least one Test-Taking Tip, which helps you prepare for a test by giving you suggestions on how to approach certain types of questions, or strategies such as how to eliminate unnecessary information. At the back of this book, you will find the answer key for each lesson. The answer to each question is provided along with a rationale for why the answer is correct. If you answer a question incorrectly, please return to the appropriate lesson and section in either the online or print Core Student Module to review the specific content.

About the *HiSET*® Social Studies Exam

The *HiSET*® Social Studies exam assesses across four content categories: History, Civics and Government, Economics, and Geography. Approximately 45% of the test is dedicated to History, 30% to Civics and Government, 15% to Economics, and approximately 10% to Geography. You may be asked to analyze and evaluate information in reading passages, primary documents, posters, cartoons, maps, graphs, tables, charts, and time lines. There are a total of 50 questions on the test, all of which are multiple choice format. Test-takers have 70 minutes to complete all questions.

All of the questions on the *HiSET*® Social Studies exam are in multiple choice format. Each multiple-choice question contains four answer choices, of which there is only one correct answer. Look for any possible answers that cannot be correct based on the information given. You may also see extraneous information in the question that is used in the answer choices. Identify and eliminate this information so you can focus on the relevant information to answer the question.

Strategies for Test Day

There are many things you should do to prepare for test day, including studying. Other ways to prepare you for the day of the test include preparing physically, arriving early, and recognizing certain strategies to help you succeed during the test. Some of these strategies are listed below.

- **Prepare physically.** Make sure you are rested both physically and mentally the day of the test. Eating a well-balanced meal will also help you concentrate while taking the text. Staying stress-free as much as possible on the day of the test will make you more likely to stayed focused than when you are stressed.

- **Arrive early.** Arrive at the testing center at least 30 minutes before the beginning of the test. Give yourself enough time to get seated and situated in the room. Keep in mind that many testing centers will not admit you if you are late.

- **Think positively.** Studies have shown that a positive attitude can help with success, although studying helps even more.

- **Relax during the test.** Stretching and deep breathing can help you relax and refocus. Try doing this a few times during the test, especially if you feel frustrated, anxious, or confused.

- **Read the test directions carefully.** Make sure you understand what the directions are asking you to do and complete the activity appropriately. If you have any questions about the test, or how to answer a specific item type using the computer, ask before the beginning of the test.

- **Know the time limit for each test.** The Social Studies portion of the test has a time limit of 70 minutes (1 hour 10 minutes). Try to work at a manageable pace. If you have extra time, go back to check your answers and finish any questions you might have skipped.

- **Have a strategy for answering questions.** For each question, read through the question prompt, identifying the important information to answer the question. If you need, reread the information provided as well as any answer choices provided.

- **Don't spend a lot of time on difficult questions.** If you are unable to answer a question or are not confident in your answer, move on and come back to it later. If you are taking the paper and pencil version of the *HiSET®* exam, you may use the scrap paper with which you are provided to keep track of questions you wish to review. If you are taking the computer-based version of the *HiSET®* exam, use the "mark and review" feature the testing software to mark the question and move on to the next question. Answer easier questions first. At the end of the test you will be able to answer and review questions you have marked, if time permits. Regardless of whether you have skipped questions or not, you should try to finish with around 10–15 minutes left so you have time to answer questions you have marked and to check all of your answers.

- **Answer every question on the test.** If you do not know the answer, try to narrow down the possible answers and then make your best educated guess. You will lose points leaving questions unanswered, but making a guess could possibly help you gain points.

Good luck with your studies, and remember: you are here because you have chosen to achieve important and exciting new goals for yourself. Every time you begin working within the materials, keep in mind that the skills you develop in *Common Core Achieve: Mastering Essential Test Readiness Skills* are not just important for passing the *HiSET®* exam; they are keys to lifelong success.

This lesson will help you understand how governments vary among countries and identify documents that contributed to American democracy. Use it with Core Lesson 1.1 *Types of Modern and Historical Governments* to reinforce and apply your knowledge.

Key Concept

Governments within a state, country, or region are responsible for establishing order, providing security, and directing public affairs.

Types of Government

Different types of government exist throughout the world at the local, state, and national levels.

Directions: Answer the following questions.

1 **Which of the following definitions fits the meaning of the term "autocracy"?**

A A form of government in which all power rests with only one person

B A form of government in which power rests with a small group of people

C A form of government in which power is inherited by a king or queen

D A form of government in which citizens vote on all issues of government

2 **How is the legislature in the United States similar to the Parliament in Canada?**

A Both are examples of direct democracy.

B Both contain representatives elected by citizens.

C Both contain a few members who hold most of the power.

D Both select the chief executive from the political party with the most seats.

3 **How does a dictatorship differ from a constitutional monarchy?**

A Monarchs have ceremonial power, whereas dictators have absolute power.

B Dictators are elected, whereas monarchs are usually born to their position.

C Monarchs are elected, whereas dictators seize power by force.

D Dictators have to follow a constitution, whereas monarchs have to obey parliament.

4 **What feature defines an oligarchy?**

A Direct rule by citizens

B Rule by a single dictator

C Rule by a small group of people

D Rule by a constitutional monarch

Test-Taking Tip

When you are answering multiple-choice questions, use the process of elimination. That is, first eliminate all answers you know are definitely incorrect. Then analyze the remaining options to determine which one is the correct answer.

Directions: Questions 5 through 7 are based on the following information.

[B]ut an oligarchy and democracy differ in this from each other, in the poverty of those who govern in the one, and the riches of those who govern in the other; for when the government is in the hands of the rich, be they few or be they more, it is an oligarchy; when it is in the hands of the poor, it is a democracy: but, as we have already said, the one will be always few, the other numerous, but both will enjoy liberty; and from the claims of wealth and liberty will arise continual disputes with each other for the lead in public affairs.

—Aristotle, *A Treatise on Government*

Is it credible that the democracy which has annihilated the feudal system and vanquished kings will respect the citizen and the capitalist? Will it stop now that it has grown so strong and its adversaries so weak? None can say which way we are going, for all terms of comparison are wanting: the equality of conditions is more complete in the Christian countries of the present day than it has been at any time or in any part of the world; so that the extent of what already exists prevents us from foreseeing what may be yet to come.

—Alexis de Tocqueville, *Democracy in America*

5 **What are Aristotle and de Tocqueville concerned about regarding democracy?**

   A The strength of oligarchies

   B The liberty of Christian countries

   C The poverty of those who govern

   D The power of the rich versus the poor

6 **According to Aristotle, when is a democracy like an oligarchy?**

   A When those in power are poor

   B When those in power are wealthy

   C When those in power are in the minority

   D When those in power are in the majority

7 **What is de Tocqueville worried about regarding the future of democracy?**

   A The feudal system will return to Christian nations.

   B Monarchies will replace democratic governments.

   C Democratic governments will overtake the world.

   D Citizens and capitalists might not be treated relatively equally.

8 **The most likely reason that writers of the Constitution did not create a direct democracy as a form of government is**

   A in direct democracies, only male citizens can vote.

   B the United States was too big to have a direct democracy.

   C individual citizens lack power in a direct democracy.

   D direct democracies tend to devolve into dictatorships.

Documents That Contributed to the Development of American Democracy

Several historical documents played an important role in the establishment of the United States government.

Directions: Answer the following questions.

9 The Declaration of Independence and the Virginia Declaration of Rights assert that

    A government draws its rightful power from the consent of the people.

    B people have a duty to change a government that is not trustworthy.

    C all citizens should be given the right to worship as they choose.

    D citizens must have a right and a means to acquire and own property.

10 Including the Bill of Rights, there are 27 amendments. What can you infer about the inclusion of an amendment process in the Constitution?

    A The authors of the Constitution could not agree on the rights to include.

    B The authors of the Constitution realized it was a flawed document.

    C An amendment process was included so the Constitution would be a flexible document and change as society changed.

    D The amendment process was included because the authors did not want a Constitution that would be changed.

11 Consider the Third Amendment to the US Constitution.

> No soldier shall, in time of peace be quartered in any house, without the consent of the owner, nor in time of war, but in a manner to be prescribed by law.

The most likely reason for adding this amendment was

    A because an active military posed a danger to the new government.

    B to balance the power between individuals and governments.

    C to convince the remaining states to ratify the Constitution.

    D because colonists were forced to house British soldiers during colonial times.

12 The first ten amendments to the Constitution are collectively known as the

    A Bill of Rights.

    B Declaration of Rights.

    C Articles of Confederation.

    D Declaration of the Rights of Man.

Directions: Questions 13 through 15 are based on the following information.

Fifteenth Amendment—The right of citizens of the United States to vote shall not be denied or abridged by the United States or by any State on account of race, color, or previous condition of servitude.

Nineteenth Amendment—The right of citizens of the United States to vote shall not be denied or abridged by the United States or by any State on account of sex.

Twenty-Fourth Amendment—The right of citizens of the United States to vote in any primary or other election for President or Vice President, for electors for President or Vice President, or for Senator or Representative in Congress, shall not be denied or abridged by the United States or any State by reason of failure to pay any poll tax or other tax.

Twenty-Sixth Amendment—The right of citizens of the United States, who are eighteen years of age or older, to vote shall not be denied or abridged by the United States or by any State on account of age.

13 The amendments to the US Constitution are listed in numerical and chronological order. Based on this information, which of the following is true? The right to vote was granted to

A white women before African American men or women.

B African American men before women of any race.

C eighteen-year-old women before eighteen-year-old men.

D African Americans before they were legally declared citizens.

14 Many citizens who were old enough to serve in the military were angered that they were not old enough to vote. Their protests resulted in which amendment?

A Fifteenth Amendment

B Nineteenth Amendment

C Twenty-Fourth Amendment

D Twenty-Sixth Amendment

15 Which amendment made voting a right for those who are impoverished?

A Fifteenth Amendment

B Nineteenth Amendment

C Twenty-Fourth Amendment

D Twenty-Sixth Amendment

16 Consider this statement from the Declaration of Independence.

> That to secure these rights, Governments are instituted among Men, deriving their just powers from the consent of the governed . . .

Which type of government does this statement describe?

A Oligarchy

B Monarchy

C Democracy

D Dictatorship

17 Like the Bill of Rights, the Magna Carta was written to

A protect the rights of those who rule.

B protect the rights of individual citizens.

C define the structure of the government.

D define the structure of the court system.

This lesson will help you understand what led to the Constitutional Convention and how compromises led to constitutional amendments. Use it with Core Lesson 1.2 *American Constitutional Democracy* to reinforce and apply your knowledge.

Key Concept

The Constitution was not met with universal approval, and had to be changed to get the new American states to approve it.

The Need for a Constitution

After the Revolutionary War, the first plan of government, the Articles of Confederation, was not strong enough for the new country.

Directions: Answer the following questions.

1 The Framers of the Articles of Confederation most likely feared a strong central government because

   A they recognized that bigger states might dominate smaller states.

   B they were concerned that a strong central government could seize property.

   C a strong central government would not have derived its power from the people.

   D they thought that a strong central government would abuse its power.

2 Under constitutionalism, which of the following is true?

   A The government's power comes from its citizens.

   B The government's power is based on a set of written rules.

   C Provisions for change within the government are unnecessary.

   D The government's power is unlimited.

3 Why did farmers take up arms against state governments during Shays's Rebellion?

   A The farmers believed that the Articles of Confederation were unfair.

   B The courts and tax collectors had begun seizing farms as repayment for debt.

   C The state governments did not support the creation of a new constitution.

   D The farmers believed that the federal government had incurred too much debt.

4 Most states included "natural rights" clauses in their constitutions. These were rights that

   A allowed each citizen to do whatever he or she wanted.

   B protected a citizen's right to not pay taxes.

   C established a true democracy in those states.

   D no government should be allowed to violate.

Test-Taking Tip

When you are answering multiple-choice questions, use the process of elimination. First eliminate all answers you know are definitely incorrect. Then analyze the remaining options to determine the correct answer.

A Nation Built on Compromise

The Constitutional Convention convened in 1787 to rewrite the rules by which the United States would work. The result was the US Constitution.

Directions: Answer the following questions.

5 Citizens retain popular sovereignty in a country by which of the following?

    A Taking part in the judicial system as jurors at trials

    B Running for office

    C Voting in federal, state, and local elections

    D Paying taxes at the federal, state, and local levels

6 A president's ability to nominate federal judges is an example of

    A checks and balances.

    B limited government.

    C popular sovereignty.

    D judicial review.

7 What did the delegates to the Constitutional Convention include in the Constitution to address their concerns about being ruled by a strong central government?

    A The Bill of Rights

    B Separation of powers

    C A judicial branch

    D A way to amend the Constitution

8 What is the role of the judicial branch of government?

    A To enforce laws

    B To carry out laws

    C To determine the constitutionality of laws

    D To pass laws

9 Shared power between the states and the national government is known as

    A judicial review.

    B federalism.

    C popular sovereignty.

    D democracy.

10 How were the rights of small states protected when the Constitution was written?

    A The federal government was given less authority over smaller states than larger states.

    B Each state received equal representation in the House of Representatives.

    C Each state received equal representation in the Senate.

    D Small states were assigned an extra representative in the Senate.

11 The Constitution was eventually ratified by how many of the original 13 states?

    A 10

    B 11

    C 12

    D 13

Directions: Questions 12 and 13 are based on the passage below.

Written by James Madison, [Federalist, No. 10] defended the form of federal government proposed by the Constitution. Critics of the Constitution argued that the proposed federal government was too large and would be unresponsive to the people.

In response, Madison explored majority rule v. minority rights in this essay. He countered that it was exactly the great number of factions and diversity that would avoid tyranny. Groups would be forced to negotiate and compromise among themselves, arriving at solutions that would respect the rights of minorities. Further, he argued that the large size of the country would actually make it more difficult for factions to gain control over others. "The influence of factious leaders may kindle a flame within their particular States, but will be unable to spread a general conflagration through the other States."

—The Bill of Rights Institute

12 **Based on the selection above, select the best definition for *faction*.**

   A   A controlling majority group in a country

   B   A leader who seeks to change the government

   C   A smaller group that disagrees with a larger group

   D   People who work for the government

13 **With which of the following statements would Madison agree regarding majority rule and minority rights?**

   A   Liberty should not be limited in order to reduce the number of factions.

   B   Liberty should be limited in order to reduce the number of factions.

   C   Majority rule sometimes means minority rights will suffer.

   D   The government should build consensus on all issues.

Directions: Answer the following questions.

14 **The first ten amendments to the Constitution are collectively known as the**

   A   Articles of Confederation.

   B   Bill of Rights.

   C   Federalist Amendments.

   D   Magna Carta.

15 **Enforcement of the nation's laws is directed by the**

   A   Executive branch.

   B   Judicial branch.

   C   Legislative branch.

   D   House of Representatives.

16 **Which of the following quotes best describes the rule of law?**

   A   "The fundamental law of the militia is, that it be created, directed and commanded by the laws, and ever for the support of the laws." —John Adams

   B   "In framing a government which is to be administered by men over men you must first enable the government to control the governed." —James Madison

   C   "For as in absolute governments the King is law, so in free countries the law ought to be king; and there ought to be no other." —Thomas Paine

   D   "A Bill of Rights is what the people are entitled to against every government, and what no just government should refuse." —Thomas Jefferson

Amending the Constitution

The United States is governed according to the rules set forth in the Constitution. The Framers of the document created a way to amend—to change or add to—the Constitution through the passage of amendments.

Directions: Answer the following questions.

17 **The first four amendments to the Constitution addressed which of the following concerns held by the colonists?**

A Unfair court procedures

B Discrimination based on race

C Power held by the states not reserved for the central government

D Basic rights violated by Britain before the Revolutionary War

18 **Which two steps are required in the process of changing, or amending, the Constitution?**

A Proposing an amendment in Congress and ratifying the amendment by a majority of states

B Passing of the amendment in the House and then passing of the amendment in the Senate

C Passing of the amendment in Congress and then by a minority of states

D Ratifying the amendment and agreement by a majority of states

19 **Consider the statement below.**

> "In framing a system which we wish to last for all ages, we should not lose sight of the changes which ages will produce."
>
> —James Madison

How is our system of government able to respond to the changes to which Madison refers?

A A presidential election is held every four years.

B New judges are constantly joining the judicial system.

C Constitutional amendments address new and evolving issues.

D The system of checks and balances enables the government to respond to new issues.

Directions: Question 20 is based on the passage below.

The Second Amendment states: *A well regulated militia, being necessary to the security of a free state, the right of the people to keep and bear arms, shall not be infringed.*

A survey was conducted by Gallup during January 14–16, 2011, in which people were asked their position on passing stronger gun laws. The survey results showed that 26% were **strongly in favor**, 23% were **in favor**, 23% were **opposed**, 27% were **strongly opposed**, and 1% had **no opinion.**

20 **What conclusion can you draw about the American public's position on gun laws from this Gallup poll?**

A Most people are in favor of stronger gun laws.

B Most people are not in favor of stronger gun laws.

C Americans are not interested in the issue of gun regulation.

D Americans are divided over whether there should be stronger gun laws.

This lesson will help you understand the power of state and federal governments and how both are structured. Use it with Core Lesson 1.3 *Structure of American Government* to reinforce and apply your knowledge.

Key Concept

The federal and state governments provide services to people, but they have unique roles and responsibilities.

The Three Branches of Government

The framers of the US Constitution created a new government that had a strong, but limited, central government divided into three branches—executive, legislative, and judicial—each with a specific set of powers.

Directions: Answer the following questions.

1 **Which of the following is the primary job of the president?**

   A   To sign or veto legislation

   B   To act as commander-in-chief

   C   To run the executive department

   D   To entertain and inform foreign diplomats

2 **Which of the following is an example of checks and balances?**

   A   The Supreme Court reviews decisions made by lower courts.

   B   The president issues a pardon to someone who has been convicted of a crime.

   C   The Congress amends a law that the Supreme Court has found to be unconstitutional.

   D   The Secretary of Energy gives the president advice, but the president does not take it.

3 **What is the primary job of the legislative branch?**

   A   To determine the constitutionality of laws

   B   To make sure that laws are carried out

   C   To pass new laws

   D   To enforce the laws

4 **How does the legislative branch exercise its checks and balances toward the executive branch?**

   A   It can override a presidential veto.

   B   It can make its own appointments to the Supreme Court.

   C   It can enter into treaties without presidential approval.

   D   It has the power to name ambassadors to foreign nations.

 Test-Taking Tip

During an exam, it often helps to take a momentary break, shut your eyes, and take a few deep breaths. It will help you clear your head and stay fresh during the exam session. Just two or three 30-second breaks can be very beneficial.

Directions: Use the chart below to help answer questions 5 and 6.

Division of Powers

Executive Branch	Legislative Branch	Judicial Branch
President	Congress	Supreme Court
• Enforces the laws • Acts as commander-in-chief of the armed forces • Appoints ambassadors, judges, and other officials • Makes treaties with other nations	• Writes the laws • Raises troops for armed forces • Decides how much money may be spent on government programs	• Interprets the laws • Reviews court decisions

5 On the basis of this chart, the executive and legislative branches of government share

A money powers.

B military powers.

C commerce powers.

D foreign policy powers.

6 According to the chart, which branch is responsible for peaceful negotiations with other countries?

A Executive Branch

B Legislative Branch

C Judicial Branch

D Both Legislative and Judicial Branches

Directions: Questions 7 through 9 are based on the following information.

To members of Congress, the president now looms large in the legislative process. He sets the national agenda and has behind him the vast knowledge and expertise of the federal bureaucracy. In this media-driven age, he speaks with one voice, as against the many of Congress, making it easier for him to command the attention of the cameras.

—Radio broadcast of Lee Hamilton, U.S. Representative to Congress from Indiana (1965–1999)

7 According to the passage, what has allowed the president to have a greater role in the legislative process?

A The media

B Former presidents

C Members of Congress

D The federal bureaucracy

8 The author of the passage implies that presidents prior to the 20th century

A did not cooperate with Congress.

B never used the media to communicate.

C did not have as much influence on legislation.

D were not supported by a federal bureaucracy.

9 Considering the years Lee Hamilton was a Congressman, how might the "media-driven age" to which he refers be different now than it was then?

A During his time in office, radio would have been the only source of media.

B During his time in office, there would have been more media outlets than there are now.

C In today's world, the emergence of social media has created an even larger audience for people to reach.

D In today's world, fewer politicians use media to reach voters.

The Power of State Government

States share some powers with the federal government; however, some powers are held only by the states.

Directions: Answer the following questions.

10 Which of the following powers is reserved for state and local governments only?

- **A** The power to levy taxes
- **B** The power to hold elections
- **C** The power to borrow money
- **D** The power to establish schools

11 Powers not specified in the Constitution are considered to be held by whom?

- **A** States
- **B** The Supreme Court
- **C** The federal government
- **D** The United Nations

Directions: Questions 12 through 14 are based on the following information.

McCulloch v. *Maryland* (1819)

In 1816 Congress established the Second National Bank to help control the amount of unregulated currency issued by state banks. Many states questioned the constitutionality of the national bank. Maryland set a precedent by requiring taxes on all banks not chartered by the state. In 1818 the State of Maryland approved legislation to impose taxes on the Second National Bank chartered by Congress.

James W. McCulloch, a federal cashier at the Baltimore branch of the US bank, refused to pay the taxes imposed by the state. Maryland filed a suit against McCulloch in an effort to collect the taxes. The Supreme Court, however, decided that the chartering of a bank was an implied power of the Constitution, under the "elastic clause," which granted Congress the authority to "make all laws which shall be necessary and proper for carrying into execution" the work of the federal government.

The proceedings posed two questions: Does the Constitution give Congress power to create a bank? And could individual states ban or tax the bank? The court decided that the federal government had the right and power to set up a federal bank and that states did not have the power to tax the federal government. Marshall ruled in favor of the federal government and concluded, "The power to tax involves the power to destroy."

12 According to the passage, the "elastic clause" gives Congress the power to set up a federal bank so that it may carry out its constitutional duty to

- **A** regulate trade between the states.
- **B** levy taxes.
- **C** coin money and regulate its value.
- **D** borrow money on the credit of the United States.

13 The power to set up a bank is shared by both the state and federal government. This is known as what type of power?

- **A** Equilateral
- **B** Concurrent
- **C** Reserved
- **D** Identical

14 Chief Justice Marshall included this statement in his decision in *McCulloch* v. *Maryland*: "The power to tax involves the power to destroy." What did Marshall mean by this statement?

- **A** The power to tax is reserved for the federal government alone.
- **B** The "elastic clause" gives Congress a power that is at times destructive.
- **C** The Constitution does not recognize the state or federal government's right to tax.
- **D** The state governments could use the power to tax to weaken the federal government.

The Structure of State Government

State governments are organized similarly to the federal government, with executive, legislative, and judicial branches.

Directions: Answer the following questions.

15 As opposed to the federal government, state governments allow citizens to exercise more direct power in their government through

   A the election of public officials.

   B financial contributions to campaigns.

   C the ability to submit laws to the legislature.

   D the right to refuse to pay taxes.

16 Citizens of a state can exercise three important powers in their state, including which of the following?

   A Impeachment

   B Assessment

   C Referendum

   D Indirect initiative

17 Which is the only state with a unicameral legislature?

   A Nebraska

   B Iowa

   C Kansas

   D Minnesota

18 If the governor of a state is equivalent to the president of the United States, which of the following offices would be equivalent to the vice president?

   A State treasurer

   B Attorney general

   C Secretary of state

   D Lieutenant governor

19 A law written by a citizen to be considered by a state legislature is called a

   A referendum.

   B direct initiative.

   C petition.

   D poll.

This lesson will help you understand how civil rights have progressed for US citizens, particularly for African Americans and women. Use it with Core Lesson 2.1 *Individual Rights and Responsibilities* to reinforce and apply your knowledge.

Key Concept

Constitutional amendments and new laws have helped extend civil rights to more people in the United States.

Civil Rights and Civil Liberties

Freedoms that are guaranteed by the United States Constitution are called civil liberties. Civil rights are the rights of full citizenship and equality under the law.

Directions: Questions 1 and 2 are based on the following information.

. . . in all capital or criminal prosecutions a man has a right to demand the cause and nature of his accusation, to be confronted with the accusers and witnesses, to call for evidence in his favor, and to a speedy trial by an impartial jury . . .

—George Mason,
Virginia Declaration of Rights,
1776

1 **George Mason's point of view regarding the rights of the accused is reflected in what Constitutional amendment?**

A   First Amendment

B   Sixth Amendment

C   Fourteenth Amendment

D   Nineteenth Amendment

2 **The word "impartial" means**

A   unbiased.

B   influenced.

C   US citizen.

D   voters.

Directions: Use the chart below to answer question 3.

Civil Liberties	Civil Rights
To vote in an election	To live wherever you choose
To speak your opinion	

3 **Which of the following best completes the chart?**

A   To have a fair trial

B   To own property

C   To access public buildings

D   To have access to a divorce

Directions: Questions 4 and 5 are based on the following information.

Congress shall make no law respecting an establishment of religion, or prohibiting the free exercise thereof; or abridging the freedom of speech, or of the press; or the right of the people peaceably to assemble, and to petition the Government for a redress of grievances.

—First Amendment to the Constitution

4 How does the Establishment Clause of the First Amendment set up "a wall of separation between church and state"?

A It prevents the government from ruling on religious matters.

B It prevents the government from endorsing a particular religion.

C It allows the government to prosecute people who establish religions.

D It allows the government to levy taxes against churches.

5 According to the passage, the term "prohibiting" means

A organizing.

B encouraging.

C preventing.

D recommending.

Directions: Questions 6 and 7 are based on the following information.

. . . [t]he person in custody must, prior to interrogation, be clearly informed that he/she has the right to remain silent, and that anything the person says will be used against that person in court; the person must be clearly informed that he/she has the right to consult with an attorney and to have that attorney present during questioning, and that, if he/she is indigent, an attorney will be provided at no cost to represent him/her.

—Chief Justice Earl Warren, delivering Supreme Court decision in *Miranda* v. *Arizona* (1966)

6 The Warren Court most likely based its decision in *Miranda* v. *Arizona* on what Constitutional amendment?

A First Amendment

B Fourth Amendment

C Fifth Amendment

D Fifteenth Amendment

7 According to the passage, the term "indigent" most likely means

A innocent.

B unable to afford.

C related to.

D under the age of 18.

 Test-Taking Tip

The more you practice reading different types of texts of different lengths, the better prepared you will be to read and understand passages presented in reading tests. A good way to practice is to read as much as you can about subjects that interest you. Not only will you become a better reader when taking a test, you will also increase your enjoyment of reading.

Civil Rights for African Americans

The end of the Civil War eliminated slavery and also extended civil rights to all males born or naturalized in America.

Directions: Answer the following questions.

8 The Supreme Court ruling in *Plessy* v. *Ferguson* (1896) stated that

   A African Americans could not be kept from running for office.

   B schools for African American children did not have to be built.

   C segregation was legal as long as facilities were "separate but equal."

   D African Americans had the equal right to own land.

9 One result of the ruling in *Plessy* v. *Ferguson* was that

   A the price of land rose dramatically in some states.

   B small "community" schools cropped up.

   C the first African American was elected to Congress.

   D Jim Crow laws were enacted in Southern states.

10 Consider the statement below.

> Any law that degrades human personality is unjust. All segregation statutes are unjust because segregation distorts the soul and damages the personality. It gives the segregator a false sense of superiority and the segregated a false sense of inferiority.
>
> —Dr. Martin Luther King, Jr.

Dr. King's point of view is most clearly reflected in

   A the Establishment Clause of the First Amendment.

   B *Plessy* v. *Ferguson*.

   C *Brown* v. *Board of Education, Topeka, Kansas*.

   D the Equal Pay Act of 1963.

Women's Rights

After the Civil War, the women who championed voting rights for African American men turned their attention toward securing the same rights for women.

Directions: Questions 11 and 12 are based on the following information.

That man over there says that women need to be helped into carriages, and lifted over ditches, and to have the best place everywhere. Nobody ever helps me into carriages, or over mud-puddles, or gives me any best place! And ain't I a woman? Look at me! Look at my arm! I have ploughed and planted, and gathered into barns, and no man could head me! And ain't I a woman? I could work as much and eat as much as a man—when I could get it—and bear the lash as well! And ain't I a woman? I have borne thirteen children, and seen most all sold off to slavery, and when I cried out with my mother's grief, none but Jesus heard me! And ain't I a woman?

        —excerpt from "Ain't I a Woman" speech made by Sojourner Truth at the Women's Rights Convention, Akron, Ohio, 1851

11 **What is the main idea of Sojourner Truth's speech?**

   A Black men and all women suffered the same ills.

   B Women are as able as men.

   C Women need special rights that are not given to men.

   D Female enslaved workers suffered more than male enslaved workers.

12 **The text of the speech indicates that, besides women's rights, Sojourner Truth would most likely have supported**

   A passage of the Fourth Amendment.

   B passage of the Thirteenth Amendment.

   C a change in custody laws.

   D a change in social customs.

Directions: Use the time line below to answer questions 13 through 15.

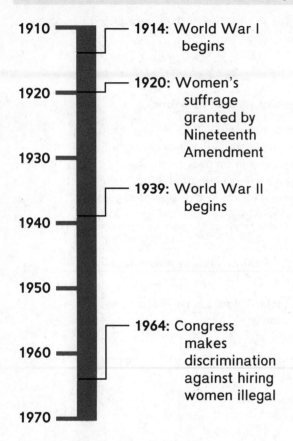

1910 — 1914: World War I begins

1920 — 1920: Women's suffrage granted by Nineteenth Amendment

1930 —

1939: World War II begins

1940 —

1950 —

1964: Congress makes discrimination against hiring women illegal

1960 —

1970 —

14 Based on this information, you can conclude that during and after World War II, women realized that they lacked equality with men in the area of

A voting rights.

B property rights.

C employment rights.

D custody rights.

15 Which of the following definitions fits the meaning of the term "suffrage" as it is used in the time line above?

A Separation of races

B Right to vote

C Guarantee of religious freedom

D Right to civil disobedience

13 Which of the following best completes the time line above?

A A law is passed that guarantees women equal facilities in college athletics.

B Women gain the right to vote in state elections.

C The Equal Rights Amendment is ratified by the states.

D Congress makes it illegal to pay men more than women for the same job.

This lesson will help you understand the role of political parties in United States politics and how interest groups and private individuals participate in our democratic society. Use it with Core Lesson 2.2 *Political Parties, Campaigns, and Elections* to reinforce and apply your knowledge.

Key Concept

People can make their views known and influence public policy through political parties and interest groups.

American Political Parties

Political parties are organizations of like-minded individuals who work to influence national policies by nominating candidates for elected office.

Directions: Questions 1 and 2 are based on the following information.

. . . there is not a liberal America and a conservative America—there is the United States of America. There is not a black America and a white America and Latino America and Asian America; there's the United States of America. The pundits like to slice-and-dice our country into Red States and Blue States; Red States for Republicans, Blue States for Democrats. But I've got news for them, too. We worship an awesome God in the Blue States, and we don't like federal agents poking around in our libraries in the Red States. We coach Little League in the Blue States and have gay friends in the Red States. There are patriots who opposed the war in Iraq and there are patriots who supported it. We are one people, all of us pledging allegiance to the stars and stripes, all of us defending the United States of America.

—Senator Barack Obama, Keynote Address,
2004 Democratic National Convention

1 **In this speech, Senator Obama was most likely trying to appeal to what group of voters?**

   A Ethnic groups

   B Religious voters

   C Independent voters

   D Veterans groups

2 **Senator Obama gave this speech at his party's national convention. A national convention has two main tasks. Which one of these two tasks did Senator Obama's speech most likely achieve?**

   A Expressing a party's beliefs

   B Forming a coalition government

   C Nominating a candidate

   D Raising campaign funds

Test-Taking Tip

Use your prior knowledge when making inferences about a passage on a test. Before reading the passage, read the title, look at any illustrations or graphics that accompany it, and skim the text for any words that are highlighted or repeated throughout. Based on these, use what you already know about words and ideas mentioned to predict what topics you expect to be discussed in the passage. While you read, combine details in the text with what you already know to make inferences and to better understand what you are reading.

Directions: Use the chart below to answer questions 3 through 5.

Third-Party Presidential Candidates		
Below are some third-party or independent candidates in the twentieth century who received a significant percentage of the vote.		
Candidate	Party	% of vote
Theodore Roosevelt (1912)	Progressive Party	27
Eugene Debs (1912)	Socialist Party	7
Robert M. LaFoliete (1924)	Progressive Party	17
George Wallace (1968)	American Independent Party	14
John B. Anderson (1980)	National Unity Campaign	7
H. Ross Perot (1992)	(Independent)	19
H. Ross Perot (1996)	Reform Party	9
Ralph Nader (2000)	Green Party	3

3 **Based on what you have learned about third parties in American politics, what can you conclude about the elections listed in the chart above?**

A Neither the Democrat nor the Republican Party held a nominating convention in these election years.

B Neither the Democrat nor the Republican nominee was able to win enough electoral votes to become president.

C Neither the Democrat nor the Republican candidate addressed a set of issues that was important to some voters.

D Neither the Democrat nor the Republican candidate was able to get enough support to form a coalition government.

4 **In 1992, H. Ross Perot ran for president as an Independent. After the election, he formed the Reform Party and ran for president as its candidate in 1996. The most likely explanation for Perot's change in affiliation is that**

A the Reform Party provided a label and a broader set of values and goals.

B he was no longer allowed to run as an independent.

C people are usually more loyal to a person than they are to a political party.

D he was the only person from the Reform Party who sought the nomination.

5 **Although third-party candidates have won a high percentage of votes, the chart shows that none has won the presidency in the 20th century. What is the most likely explanation for this?**

A Third-party members donate more money to political campaigns than members of the major parties.

B Third-party candidates have less money than candidates representing the two major parties.

C Third-party candidates are less experienced at campaigning than Democrats and Republicans.

D Third party candidates usually focus on one or a few major issues.

Political Campaigns and Elections

Political campaigns give voters information about candidates and issues, but the responsibility for investigating, understanding, and making informed decisions resides with each voter.

Directions: Questions 6 and 7 are based on the political cartoon below.

6 **What does the image of President Theodore Roosevelt pushing the elephant up the hill most likely symbolize?**

   A It symbolizes the push to protect the habitats of the African elephant.

   B It symbolizes the struggle that presidents must endure while in office.

   C It symbolizes the dilemma of using elephants to help build the Panama Canal.

   D It symbolizes Roosevelt's resolve to get Republicans to back the Panama Canal.

7 **What characteristic(s) allows you to conclude that the image is a political cartoon (as opposed to another kind of artwork)?**

   A The image is a realistic depiction of political events.

   B The image was drawn by a prominent political figure.

   C The image combines symbols and caricatures to make a point.

   D The image is a crudely drawn pencil sketch.

Directions: Answer the following question.

8 **Most campaigns for national office cost millions of dollars. The main reason for this is that**

   A candidates compete for the donations of wealthy contributors.

   B some states mandate a minimum that a campaign has to spend.

   C lengthy campaigns require money to convey the candidate's message.

   D the candidates are not required to spend their own money on the campaign.

Directions: Questions 9 and 10 are based on the chart below.

2000 Presidential Election				
Party	Candidate	Electoral Votes	Popular Votes	% of Popular Vote
Republican	George W. Bush	271	50,455,156	47.9
Democrat	Albert Gore, Jr.	266	50,992,335	48.4
Green	Ralph Nader	0	2,882,738	2.7

9 In presidential elections, how does the popular vote differ from the electoral vote?

   A The popular vote, which is the number of votes cast by citizens, determines the outcome of elections; the electoral vote is symbolic.

   B The electoral vote is determined by electors of each state; the popular vote is the total number of votes cast by citizens.

   C The electoral vote is cast by senators and representatives in each state; the popular vote is the total number of votes cast by qualified voters.

   D The popular vote is made by the legislatures of each state; the electoral vote is determined by each state's electors.

10 In 2000, the outcome of voting in Florida helped determine the outcome of the presidential election. This was most likely because

   A one political party significantly outspent the other in the state, leading to victory.

   B all Florida's electoral votes were awarded to Bush, who won the state's popular vote.

   C voters in other time zones were influenced by the outcome of voting in Florida.

   D Florida's population was large enough to tip the popular vote in Bush's favor.

The Influence of Interest Groups

Interest groups influence the political process through public advocacy, by campaigning during elections, and by donating money to candidates.

Directions: Questions 11 and 12 are based on the following information.

. . . we are expected to govern with integrity, good will, clear convictions, and a servant's heart. I pledge to all Americans that I will carry myself in this spirit as vice president of the United States. This was the spirit that brought me to the governor's office, when I took on the old politics as usual in Juneau . . . when I stood up to the special interests, the lobbyists, big oil companies, and the good-ol' boys network.

           —Governor Sarah Palin, 2008 Republican National Convention Address

11 Which of the following definitions fits the meaning of the term "lobbyists"?

   A An organized group who share common values and goals

   B People whose job is to influence public officials toward a particular opinion

   C People who work together to raise money for a particular political candidate

   D A group with common concerns who work together to sway government policy

12 Why do you think Governor Palin made a point of mentioning her opposition to lobbyists?

   A Lobbyists nominate and campaign for candidates for elected office.

   B Lobbyists often testify at government hearings for or against proposed laws.

   C Lobbyists represent only Democrat candidates or liberal interest groups.

   D Lobbyists charge high fees for their services and often represent wealthy interests.

This lesson will help you define and identify examples of public policy and describe how public policies are made. Use it with Core Lesson 2.3 *Contemporary Public Policy* to reinforce and apply your knowledge.

Key Concept

Actions taken by the government to address concerns of the voting public are known as public policies.

What Is Contemporary Public Policy?

One of the key jobs of the government is to create policies that address and solve problems that affect its citizens.

Directions: Questions 1 through 3 are based on the information below.

The Preamble to the United States Constitution identifies a set of national policy goals that contemporary administrations continue to strive for.

> We the People of the United States, in Order to form a more perfect Union, establish Justice, insure domestic Tranquility, provide for the common defense, promote the general Welfare, and secure the Blessings of Liberty to ourselves and our Posterity, do ordain and establish this Constitution for the United States of America.

1 Based on information in the passage, what is the best definition of the word "domestic"?

A Comfortable

B Household

C Internal

D Supportive

2 What is the best definition of the word "posterity" as it is used in the passage?

A Other countries

B To be prosperous

C Future generations

D Within the United States

3 The Preamble declares that

A all men are created equal.

B the power of the government comes from the people.

C there is no higher power in the land.

D Congress shall hold all legislative powers.

✔ Test-Taking Tip

When you are answering vocabulary questions, remember that the correct answer is not always the primary dictionary definition. Combine the context clues given to you in the passage with what you know about the author's purpose to help you determine the intended meaning of the word.

Directions: Answer the following questions.

4 Although state and local governments write public policies, the federal government must write federal public policies to

- **A** exert control over state and local governments.
- **B** follow the guidelines set out in the Constitution.
- **C** establish laws that everyone in the nation must follow.
- **D** create examples for state and local governments to follow.

5 Rules or guidelines that apply to a specific institution would best be classified as which of the following?

- **A** Public policy
- **B** School policy
- **C** Contemporary policy
- **D** Economic policy

6 Which is an example of public policy?

- **A** A campaign sign
- **B** Prohibition of firearms in a theatre
- **C** State sales tax rate
- **D** Amount a store owner must pay an employee

7 Who is responsible for implementing public policy?

- **A** Congress
- **B** Government agencies
- **C** Special interest groups
- **D** Supreme Court

8 Which of the following public policies would best be described as a public safety policy?

- **A** Seatbelts must be worn by all passengers in a moving vehicle.
- **B** Trucks cannot exceed posted weight limits on public highways.
- **C** All vehicles must pass an emissions test before being issued a license plate.
- **D** Drivers must carry medical liability coverage through their auto insurance carrier.

9 Which level of government would determine the public policy outlining registrations for selective service?

- **A** City
- **B** County
- **C** State
- **D** Federal

How National Policy Is Made

Establishing national policy is a complex process that begins with identifying a problem.

Directions: Use the flow chart below to help answer questions 10 through 12.

Policy-Making Process

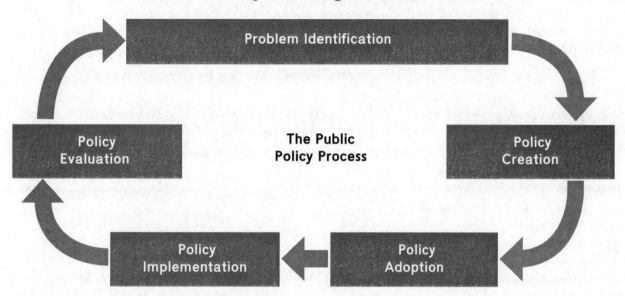

10 **What does the shape of this flow chart tell you about the policy-making process?**

   A By law, government policies can only last one year and have to be renewed.

   B Any policy solution to one problem will always cause another problem.

   C Policy-based solutions to problems are never really successful.

   D Shaping and refining public policy is an ongoing process.

11 **Which step in this process would most likely involve the participation of Congress?**

   A Policy adoption

   B Policy evaluation

   C Policy formation

   D Policy implementation

12 **Suppose the Department of Health and Human Services implemented a policy of providing free flu shots to citizens. Which of the following steps would most likely follow the implementation step in the public policy process?**

   A Health care advocates would work with lawmakers to shape the policy.

   B Congress would pass a law authorizing the distribution of free flu shots.

   C Public advocacy groups would identify a sharp rise in the number of flu fatalities.

   D Medical researchers would examine the benefits of or problems with the program.

Influences on Public Policy

The government makes public policy, but citizens, special interest groups, and lobbyists also influence public policy.

Directions: Questions 13 through 16 are based on the information below.

It is said that lobbying itself is an evil and a danger. We agree that lobbying by personal contact may be an evil and a potential danger to the best in legislative processes. It is said that indirect lobbying by the pressure of public opinion on the Congress is an evil and a danger. That is not an evil; it is a good, the healthy essence of the democratic process.

—US Court of Appeals Ruling in *Rumely* v. *United States*, 1952

13 According to the passage, which of the following best describes the process of lobbying?

A Raising awareness about key issues to help voters

B Persuading public officials to adopt particular positions

C Monitoring public officials to make sure they are not taking bribes

D Electing officials who support policies that help the general public

14 According to this passage, what lobbying practice might be considered "a potential danger to the best in legislative processes"?

A Giving testimony before Congress

B Preparing informational reports for lawmakers

C Hiring a public relations firm to promote an issue

D Personally buying lunch or dinner for government officials

15 This passage shows that citizens can indirectly influence public policy by

A sending a lobbyist to Congress.

B evaluating the effectiveness of policies.

C demanding change from elected officials.

D buying an expensive gift for an elected official.

16 Similar to lobbyists, special interest groups also try to influence public policy. Which of the following issues would most likely be taken up by a special interest group?

A Campaign finance reform

B Increasing voter registration

C Preventing texting while driving

D Relaxing health care regulations

This lesson will help you understand the causes of the American Revolution, identify documents that shaped US democratic traditions, summarize provisions of the Articles of Confederation, and understand how and why the Constitution was developed. Use it with Core Lesson 3.1 *American Revolution* to reinforce and apply your knowledge.

Key Concept

After defeating the British, the new United States established a democratic government built on a foundation of English laws and government.

English Colonies in America

British colonies were established in North American beginning in the late sixteenth century. Colonies in Virginia and New England provided English men and women a place to start a new life. Some sought religious freedom, and others sought economic gain. In each case, the settlements established rules and selected leaders to govern the colonies.

Directions: Questions 1 through 4 are based on the information below.

Having undertaken . . . a voyage to plant the first colony in [North America], do . . . covenant and combine ourselves together into a civil body politic, for our better ordering and preservation . . . and by virtue hereof to enact, constitute and frame such just and equal laws, ordinances, acts, constitutions and offices, from time to time as shall be thought most meet and convenient for the general good of the Colony . . .

—The Mayflower Compact

1   What was the purpose of this document?

A   To authorize Sir Walter Raleigh to set up a colony in North America

B   To explain why the Pilgrims broke with the Church of England

C   To establish the rules by which the Pilgrims would govern themselves

D   To give the Pilgrims large portions of land in Massachusetts

2   How were the settlers who created this document similar to the Puritans who settled the Massachusetts Bay Colony?

A   Both sought to get rich selling America's natural resources to England.

B   Both established a government based on direct democracy.

C   Both were established for the promotion of one set of religious ideals.

D   Neither was successful at establishing a long-term settlement.

3   This document is an early example of a

A   constitution.

B   charter.

C   law.

D   bill of rights.

4   What is the definition of the word "colony" as it is used in this passage?

A   A religious organization

B   A market for another country's goods

C   A voyage of discovery

D   A land controlled by another nation

The American Revolution

As Britain's empire in America grew, so did the expenses for governing colonies so far away. The costs of providing an army and material goods put a strain on England's economy. Taxes and other policies set forth by the King and Parliament were deemed unfair by many colonists. They felt no one in England was representing their cause before the governing bodies.

Directions: Questions 5–7 are based on the information below.

Let these *truths* be indelibly impressed on our minds—*that* we *cannot be* HAPPY, *without being* FREE—that we cannot be free, *without being secure in our property*—that *we* cannot be secure in our property, *if, without our consent, others may, as by right, take it away*—that *taxes imposed on us by parliament,* do thus take it away—that *duties laid for the sole purpose of raising money,* are taxes—that *attempts* to lay such duties *should be instantly and firmly opposed*—that this opposition can never be effectual, *unless it is the united effort of these . . .*

—excerpt from "Letter XII," *Letters from a Farmer in Pennsylvania*
by John Dickinson, 1768

5 **Dickinson was most likely writing in opposition to which of the following?**

   A The Townshend Acts

   B The American Revolution

   C The Boston Massacre

   D The Continental Congress

6 **Many colonists responded to the taxes mentioned in Dickinson's letter by participating in**

   A attacks on troops.

   B the burning of their fields.

   C the Continental Congress.

   D boycotts.

7 **What happened as a result of the Boston Tea Party?**

   A King George III declared war on the colonies.

   B Parliament repealed the Stamp Act.

   C British troops fired on protesters in Boston.

   D Parliament passed new restrictive laws.

✓ Test-Taking Tip

The text features that you use to determine the sequence of events can also help you find the correct answer in a test passage more quickly. When you first read a passage, make a mental note of any section headings that are used to organize the passage. Later, when you read the questions, notice whether the question tells you where in the passage to look for the answer. If it does, go straight to that section and make sure your answer corresponds to the information found in that section.

Directions: Questions 8 and 9 are based on the information below.

We therefore beseech your Majesty, that your royal authority and influence may be graciously interposed to procure us relief from our afflicting fears and jealousies . . . and to settle peace through every part of our Dominions . . . and that, in the mean time, measures may be taken for preventing the further destruction of the lives of your Majesty's subjects; and that such statutes as more immediately distress any of your Majesty's Colonies, may be repealed.

8 **This passage was most likely taken from the**

   A Declaration of Independence.

   B Olive Branch Petition.

   C Mayflower Compact.

   D Articles of Confederation.

9 **The purpose of this document was to**

   A protest over the Boston Massacre.

   B apologize for the Boston Tea Party.

   C overturn the Stamp Act and the Townshend Acts.

   D attempt a truce after the Battles of Lexington and Concord.

Directions: Questions 10 and 11 are based on the information below.

The war with France greatly increased Britain's territory in North America. It also created problems. The war nearly doubled Britain's national debt. Although nearly broke, Britain had to pay for additional soldiers to defend the new territory. The British government insisted that the colonists should help keep the peace and pay part of the cost of defense. The colonists were forced to pay the salaries of soldiers, feed them, and provide them with housing. In 1764, the British Parliament placed import duties, or fees, on sugar and other products shipped into the colonies. In 1765, it taxed legal documents and other printed matter.

10 **Which sentence states the central idea of this passage?**

   A The war nearly doubled Britain's national debt.

   B The British government insisted that the colonists should help keep the peace and pay part of the cost of defense.

   C The colonists were forced to pay the salaries of soldiers, feed them, and provide them with housing.

   D In 1765, it taxed legal documents and other printed matter.

11 **What was the cause and effect of British action in the 1760s?**

   A Because Britain could not afford the additional soldiers needed to defend the new territory, the British government insisted that the colonists pay part of the cost of defense.

   B Because the colonists were forced to pay for soldiers' food and lodging, the British Parliament placed import duties on products shipped to the colonies.

   C Because Britain's territory in North America increased, the British Parliament received more income from duties.

   D Because the colonists paid for soldiers' food and lodging, the British Parliament began taxing legal documents and other printed materials.

The Confederation Period

Recognizing the weaknesses of the Articles of Confederation, Congress convened a Constitutional Convention, which produced the US Constitution.

Directions: Answer the following questions.

12 Delegates to the Constitutional Convention settled on the Great Compromise because it

   A   did not provide for three branches of government.

   B   gave each state equal representation in the Senate.

   C   did not include the ideas of the Federalists.

   D   gave Congress too little power.

13 What basic right did the colonists believe was violated by the Stamp Act?

   A   The right to practice a religion without discrimination

   B   The right to a free press

   C   The right to own weapons and protect themselves

   D   The right to be taxed only by elected representatives

14 The Articles of Confederation did not give the federal government the power to impose taxes. Why was this a problem?

   A   The federal government was unable to print money.

   B   The federal government needed money to build roads.

   C   The federal government was not able to pay off the national debt.

   D   Each state had different taxation laws.

15 What is one way that the Articles of Confederation differed from the new Constitution?

   A   Under the Articles, the states held many powers, but under the Constitution, they have few.

   B   Under the Articles, Congress had the power to tax, but under the Constitution, Congress lacks this power.

   C   Under the Articles, the legislative branch had one house, but under the Constitution, the legislative branch has two houses.

   D   Under the Articles, the president holds has the power to declare war, but under the Constitution, the Congress holds this power.

16 On what central idea did the Great Compromise differ from the Virginia Plan?

   A   Congress would now have the power to declare war and make peace.

   B   The federal government would consist of three branches.

   C   The legislature was given the power to coin and borrow money.

   D   State population would determine representation in the House of Representatives.

This lesson will help you understand how the United States grew geographically, identify the causes and consequences of the War of 1812, and explain how westward expansion affected US Native American policy. Use it with Core Lesson 3.2 *A New Nation* to reinforce and apply your knowledge.

Key Concept

After the Revolutionary War, the United States endured conflicts within and struggled with other countries as well.

The Growth of the Nation

The expansion of the new United States was aided by the Northwest Ordinance of 1787 and the newly ratified Constitution, which created a federal government with a much stronger executive branch than that of the Articles of Confederation and a new president, George Washington.

Directions: Questions 1 and 2 are based on the information below.

So soon as there shall be five thousand free male inhabitants of full age in the district, upon giving proof thereof to the governor, they shall receive authority, with time and place, to elect a representative from their counties or townships to represent them in the general assembly . . .

1 **This passage is most likely taken from the**

  A United States Constitution.

  B Articles of Confederation.

  C Treaty of Paris.

  D Northwest Ordinance of 1787.

2 **Which definition fits the meaning of the term "township" as it is used in the passage?**

  A A gift of land from one nation to another

  B An area of land controlled by a government

  C An area of land whose borders are unclear

  D Land that is settled by a group of people

Directions: Answer the following questions.

3 **How did the Land Ordinance of 1785 initiate a sequence of events that led to the admission of five states to the Union?**

  A It allowed settlers to create governments.

  B It prohibited the taxation of land in the Northwest Territory.

  C It made land available for a low price, attracting many settlers.

  D It set up law enforcement agencies, easing fears of landowners.

4 **What was the significance of the Lewis and Clark Expedition?**

  A It allowed the army to secure the borders of the Louisiana Purchase.

  B It prevented the British from claiming the Louisiana Purchase lands.

  C It established the Mississippi River as the main shipping route for goods.

  D It provided the government with knowledge about western lands.

Directions: Use the chart below to answer questions 5 and 6.

Roles and Responsibilities of the Executive Departments

Department	Leader's Title	Main Area of Responsibility
State Department	Secretary of State	dealing with other nations
Treasury Department	Secretary of the Treasury	looking after the nation's finances
War Department	Secretary of War	defending the nation

5 The offices described in this chart were created by

   A an act of Congress.

   B an article of the Constitution.

   C presidential appointment.

   D popular vote.

6 Although Jay's Treaty eased tensions with Great Britain in 1794, it was not widely popular because

   A British troops would not withdraw from American forts.

   B it did not address all the problems between the United States and Britain.

   C most Congressmen favored sending Thomas Jefferson to negotiate the treaty.

   D it did not open the Mississippi River to American trade.

Directions: Questions 7 and 8 are based on the following information.

Louisiana Purchase Treaty (1803)

Robert Livingston and James Monroe closed on the largest real estate deal of the millennium when they signed the Louisiana Purchase Treaty in Paris on April 30, 1803. They were authorized to pay France up to $10 million for the port of New Orleans and the Floridas. When offered the entire territory of Louisiana—an area larger than Great Britain, France, Germany, Italy, Spain and Portugal combined—the American negotiators swiftly agreed to a price of $15 million.

Although President Thomas Jefferson was a strict interpreter of the Constitution who wondered whether the US Government was authorized to acquire new territory, he was also a visionary who dreamed of an "empire for liberty" that would stretch across the entire continent. As Napoleon threatened to take back the offer, Jefferson squelched whatever doubts he had and prepared to occupy a land of unimaginable riches.

7 Why would a strict interpretation of the Constitution have prevented Thomas Jefferson from moving forward with the Louisiana Purchase?

   A It would have kept him from asking Congress to raise taxes to pay for the land.

   B It would have kept him from acquiring the land because there was no specific provision for this action in the Constitution.

   C It would have required him to get approval from each of the states before proceeding with this acquisition.

   D It would have kept him from entering into a treaty with a foreign country.

8 What did Jefferson consider more important than constitutionality in making this decision?

   A His popularity with the American people

   B Providing for future growth of the nation

   C Eradicating slavery in the new territory

   D Removing all foreign landowners from America

The War of 1812

Issues with Great Britain continued for several years after the American Revolution ended, and soon war again became inevitable.

Directions: Answer the following questions.

9 **Which event happened first?**

   A British soldiers marched into Washington, D.C., and set fire to the White House.

   B A thousand militiamen defeated Tecumseh's men at the Battle of Tippecanoe.

   C War Hawks Henry Clay of Kentucky and John C. Calhoun were elected to Congress.

   D Two thousand British soldiers were killed at the Battle of New Orleans.

10 **What is one factor that contributed to the United States' involvement in the War of 1812?**

   A They wanted to open New Orleans to American trade.

   B They wanted closer relations and expanded trade with the British.

   C France and England were forcing Americans to serve on their ships.

   D They wanted to be allowed to ship their produce down the Mississippi River.

11 **Why was the Treaty of Paris considered favorable to the United States?**

   A It ended the war with Britain.

   B It gave the United States a large amount of land.

   C It opened the Northwest Territory to settlement.

   D It created a way to add new states to the confederation.

12 **Which statement best supports the idea that the Battle of New Orleans was unnecessary?**

   A The British attacked and burned Washington, D.C.

   B The war ended with the Treaty of Ghent.

   C The British surrendered when they failed to take Baltimore.

   D Britain agreed to give the United States its North American territory.

13 **Which of the following was an outcome of the War of 1812?**

   A An upsurge in American nationalism

   B The signing of Jay's Treaty

   C Increased tensions with Spain

   D The establishment of a new American navy

Manifest Destiny

In the early 1800s, Americans were angry with the British for impressing American sailors and for taking American ships. On June 18, 1812, Congress declared war against Britain. In 1815, the Treaty of Ghent ended the war. Britain and the United States agreed to restore any territories taken during the war.

Directions: Questions 14 through 16 are based on the following information.

The whole continent of North America appears to be destined by Divine Providence to be peopled by one *nation*, speaking one language, professing one general system of religious and political principles, and accustomed to one general tenor of social usages and customs. For the common happiness of them all, for their peace and prosperity, I believe it is indispensable that they should be associated in one federal Union.

—John Quincy Adams

14 In this quote, John Quincy Adams is expressing an idea that became known as

A   the Union Proclamation.

B   the Land Ordinance.

C   Westward Expansion.

D   Manifest Destiny.

15 Which event can be seen as a direct result of the beliefs espoused by Adams?

A   Jay's Treaty

B   The War of 1812

C   The annexation of Texas

D   The Battle of Tippecanoe

16 In 1828, Andrew Jackson ordered the removal of the Cherokee people from their land in Georgia, in spite of the fact that he was told he could not do this by

A   the state of Georgia.

B   Congress.

C   the Supreme Court.

D   American settlers.

 Test-Taking Tip

Some test items ask about specific words or phrases, paragraphs, or sections of a passage. Before answering a question about a text detail, reread the related sentence or paragraph, whether or not the item directs you to reread it. As you reread, focus on what the question is about. For example, if the item is about the meaning of a word, think about how the word is used as you reread.

This lesson will help you understand the causes and effects of the Civil War. It will also help you analyze a writer's point of view and his or her use of persuasive language. Use it with Core Lesson 3.3 *Civil War and Reconstruction* to reinforce and apply your knowledge.

Key Concept

To keep the country together, the North was willing to go to war, but the war was about much more than the preservation of the Union. It was about the abolition of slavery as well.

Slavery in the United States

The institution of slavery arrived in North America almost at the same time as the first settlers in 1619. In the two centuries that followed, slavery grew to become an essential part of the South's economy. As it did, many northerners, appalled by its human cost, began the movement to end slavery.

Directions: Answer the following questions.

1 **The triangular trade referred to**

   A   the exportation of cotton, rice, and tobacco from the South to Britain.

   B   the route that brought enslaved Africans to the colonies.

   C   the path taken by indentured servants, from Europe to servitude to freedom.

   D   the policy of avoiding tariffs by exporting goods to the Caribbean.

2 **Which of the following groups would most likely have supported the expansion of slavery?**

   A   Poor farmers

   B   Factory owners

   C   Wealthy planters

   D   Newspaper publishers

3 **Why did plantation owners in the South prefer to use enslaved workers instead of indentured servants?**

   A   It was less expensive to use an indentured servant than an enslaved person.

   B   It was expensive to train new workers when indentured servants ran away.

   C   Indentured servants had to be given room, board, and other benefits.

   D   Indentured servants had to be released from their contract once they married.

4 **What was transported from the colonies to Africa on the triangular trade route?**

   A   Sugar

   B   Molasses

   C   Rum

   D   Enslaved people

Directions: Use the map below to help answer questions 5 through 8.

The Missouri Compromise

- Closed to slavery by Missouri Compromise
- Open to slavery by Missouri Compromise
- Free states and territories
- Slave states

Vote of U.S. Senators on the Missouri Compromise
For: 24   Against: 20
Note that North Carolina and South Carolina split their vote.

5 Which of the following best explains why it was so important to opponents of slavery that Missouri not enter the Union as a slave state?

A   Missouri had a higher population of enslaved people than any other territory.

B   Most of the country's enslaved workers were purchased in markets in Missouri.

C   They did not believe that Missouri should have the same rights as the original states.

D   Its entry would upset the balance between the slave and free states in the Senate.

6 Why did Maine not have a vote?

A   Maine was part of Massachusetts during this time.

B   Maine was a territory and could not vote.

C   Maine abstained from the vote.

D   Only states in the south voted.

7 Which other state was created as a result of Missouri's admission to the Union?

A   Michigan

B   Maine

C   Louisiana

D   Oregon

8 Which area became closed to slavery by the Missouri Compromise?

A   Oregon Territory

B   Unorganized Territory

C   New Spain

D   Michigan Territory

 Test-Taking Tip

Before answering a question about a map, take time to analyze the information shown. If there is a map key, make sure you understand what each symbol represents and how the information is related to the map.

Civil War

In 1861, sectional conflict erupted into a full-scale Civil War, as eleven states seceded from the Union.

Directions: Questions 9 and 10 are based on the information below.

In *your* hands, my dissatisfied fellow-countrymen, and not in *mine,* is the momentous issue of civil war. The Government will not assail *you.* You can have no conflict without being yourselves the aggressors. *You* have no oath registered in heaven to destroy the Government, while I shall have the most solemn one to "preserve, protect, and defend it."

I am loath to close. We are not enemies, but friends. We must not be enemies. Though passion may have strained it must not break our bonds of affection. The mystic chords of memory, stretching from every battlefield and patriot grave to every living heart and hearthstone all over this broad land, will yet swell the chorus of the Union, when again touched, as surely they will be, by the better angels of our nature.

—Abraham Lincoln, First Inaugural Address

9 **Which of the following best explains why Lincoln stressed that the Union would not provoke a civil war?**

A Lincoln was not confident in the North's military leadership.

B Lincoln did not want to alienate slave states that had stayed in the Union.

C Lincoln still thought that the Missouri Compromise would settle the issue.

D Lincoln knew that the northern economy depended on southern cotton.

10 **Lincoln's speech is characterized by his use of**

A patriotic appeals.

B economic appeals.

C persuasive language.

D descriptive language.

Directions: Answer the following questions.

11 **From the beginning, the North's strategy was to**

A starve the South of food and supplies until they surrendered.

B lay siege to Southern farmland, burning everything.

C capture the Confederate capital and end the war quickly.

D enlist the aid of Great Britain and France against the South.

12 **What was one major advantage that the South had during the Civil War?**

A Familiarity with battlegrounds

B More factories and materials

C Naval superiority

D More men of military age

Reconstruction

The period after the Civil War is known as Reconstruction, because it was necessary to rebuild the Union and the various forms of destruction caused by the war itself.

Directions: Answer the following questions.

13 **Which sentence best explains why President Johnson required ex-Confederates to swear loyalty to the Union before they could be pardoned?**

A Johnson was planning to rebuild the US military with Civil War veterans.

B After the Civil War, every citizen was required to take a loyalty oath.

C The loyalty oaths helped ensure Johnson's personal safety after Lincoln's assassination.

D Johnson did not want the ex-Confederates to take up arms against the Union again.

14 **While the Civil War began as a means to keep the United States unified, as the war progressed, and especially after the issuance of the Emancipation Proclamation, what became a new goal for the US?**

A The punishment of Confederate leaders

B The acquisition of new territory

C The liberation of enslaved people

D A return to the prewar status quo

Directions: Questions 15 through 18 are based on the information below.

Section 1. Neither slavery nor involuntary servitude, except as a punishment for crime whereof the party shall have been duly convicted, shall exist within the United States, or any place subject to their jurisdiction.

15 **This excerpt is most likely taken from the**

A Thirteenth Amendment.

B Fourteenth Amendment.

C Fifteenth Amendment.

D Sixteenth Amendment.

16 **Many Southern states responded to this amendment by passing**

A new amendments.

B loyalty oaths.

C black codes.

D property statutes.

17 **As a result of an economic downturn in the 1870s,**

A freed African Americans began working as sharecroppers.

B Radical Republicans passed measures to restart the economy.

C Congress began to impose stricter penalties on the South.

D many Americans shifted their attention away from Reconstruction.

18 **According to this law, indentured servitude was still permissible under which condition?**

A Only in areas outside of the United States

B In areas that were under the jurisdiction of the United States

C As punishment for a crime in which someone is found guilty

D In the Oregon Territory

This lesson will help you understand why immigrants came to America, identify where they settled, and understand how they were received. Use it with Core Lesson 3.4 *European Settlement and Population of the Americas* to reinforce and apply your knowledge.

Key Concept

As immigrants came to America, they settled in cities and spread throughout the growing West.

The Growth of Immigration

The United States not only grew geographically in the period from 1820 to 1920, but it also grew in population due to the more than 33 million immigrants who moved to the United States from other countries.

Directions: Answer the following questions.

1 Poverty and lack of jobs are examples of

  A push factors.

  B pull factors.

  C immigration.

  D trade.

2 Which of the following statements would be appropriate to include in a summary of the section titled "The Growth of Immigration"?

  A Most European immigrants became farm workers.

  B Immigrants came from Europe, China, Japan, and Mexico.

  C Men took jobs as bricklayers, carpenters, and street vendors.

  D Most people were happy to be able to live in the United States.

3 What often caused an immigrant to settle in an East Coast port city rather than continuing to travel west?

  A illness

  B lack of money

  C family obligations

  D religious persecution

4 What overall effect did immigrants have on American industries?

  A Their labor helped the nation's industries grow and prosper.

  B Their knowledge introduced new technologies to American industries.

  C Their employment took factory jobs away from American citizens.

  D Their ability to work fast sped up production in factories around the nation.

Directions: Use the map to help answer questions 5 through 8.

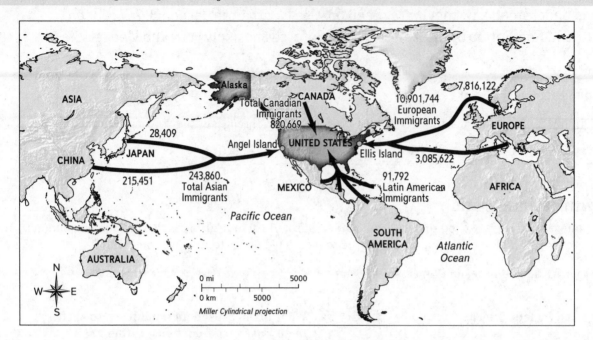

5 **Based on the numbers of immigrants as shown on this map, what region was the source of the largest numbers of immigrants to the United States during this period?**

A Asia

B Southern Europe

C Northern Europe

D Canada

6 **Based on the information in this map, you can conclude that the problem of overcrowding was most pronounced in the**

A northeast.

B west.

C Midwest.

D south.

7 **Based on where they entered the United States as shown on the map, most Latin Americans immigrants during this period most likely worked as**

A factory workers in Detroit or Chicago.

B railroad construction workers in the west.

C carpenters in the northeast.

D farmers in the southwest.

8 **Which of the following was a "push factor" that led to the increase in immigration illustrated in the map above?**

A Religious freedom

B Democracy

C Economic opportunity

D Poverty

 Test-Taking Tip

When you are answering questions involving a map, make sure you read the question first, so you can know what to look for when you study the map.

Life in America

By the end of the 19th century, more than half of all Americans were living in cities instead of on farms, encouraging a rise of poor living conditions and three distinct social classes.

Directions: Questions 9 through 12 are based on the information below.

Be a little careful, please! The hall is dark and you might stumble over the children pitching pennies back there. Not that it would hurt them; kicks and cuffs are their daily diet. They have little else. Here where the hall turns and dives into utter darkness is a step, and another, another. A flight of stairs. You can feel your way, if you cannot see it. Close? Yes!…That was a woman filling her pail by the hydrant you just bumped against. The sinks are in the hallway, t hat all the tenants may have access—and all be poisoned alike by their summer stenches. Hear the pump squeak!…In summer, when a thousand thirsty throats pant for a cooling drink in this block, it is worked in vain. But the saloon, whose open door you passed in the hall, is always there. The smell of it has followed you up. Here is a door. Listen! That short hacking cough, that tiny, helpless wail—what do they mean?

—excerpt from *How the Other Half Lives* by Jacob Riis, 1890

9 The author of this passage is most likely describing life in a

A   city center.

B   suburb.

C   tenement house.

D   farm.

10 This passage shows that one of the greatest dangers facing immigrants was

A   gang violence.

B   poor sanitation.

C   political corruption.

D   unsafe working conditions.

11 The "other half" to whom Riis is referring to in the title of this passage is most likely the

A   poor working class.

B   middle class.

C   wealthy.

D   upper class.

12 What would have been the most likely push factor within the United States to draw people to move from the farm to live in cities?

A   The opportunity to live near the city center

B   Advancements in farming technology

C   Growth of industry

D   Improvements in transportation

Discrimination Against Immigrants

Adapting to life in America was not easy for many immigrants, and their differences often made them targets of discrimination.

Directions: Use the graph to answer questions 13 through 17.

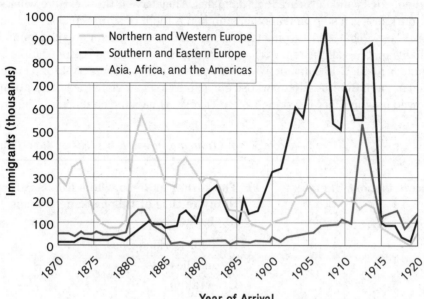

Immigration to the United States, 1870–1920

13 **Which of the following groups was most opposed to the increase in immigration illustrated in the chart above?**

  A Women

  B Catholics

  C Progressives

  D Nativists

14 **Which statement best explains why some Americans opposed this new wave of immigration?**

  A Immigrants from southern and eastern Europe had different religions and traditions.

  B Immigrants tended to push native-born citizens out of the city centers.

  C Immigrants from Asia and Eastern Europe were opposed to democratic institutions.

  D Immigrants built new factories that caused pollution and unsafe working conditions.

15 **Which of the following best explains the decline in Asian, African, and Latin American immigration between 1880 and 1885?**

  A The Progressive Movement

  B The Chinese Exclusion Act

  C The Spanish-American War

  D The Mexican Revolution

16 **To provide aid and services to this new influx of immigrants, reformers such as Jane Addams established**

  A city centers.

  B tenement houses.

  C barrios.

  D settlement houses.

17 **During which five-year period did the steepest drop in immigration from Southern and Eastern Europe occur?**

  A 1880–1885

  B 1890–1895

  C 1910–1915

  D 1915–1920

This lesson will help you identify the causes of World War I and its effects on Europe and the United States, and understand how and why the League of Nations was formed. Use it with Core Lesson 4.1 *World War I* to reinforce and apply your knowledge.

Key Concept

World War I resulted from alliances being formed throughout the world.

The United States Becomes a World Power

By the 1890s, nationalism and imperialism were two sides of the coin that made the United States a nation to be respected before the advent of World War I.

Directions: Questions 1 through 3 are based on the information below.

The Spanish-American War grew out of the American public's growing desire to expand American territory and interests and out of a general "war fever."

Several of the larger American newspapers began to capitalize on the Cuban struggle for independence from Spain, sensationalizing abuses Spanish military forces were committing against the Cubans.

Public outrage reached its peak with the sinking of the battleship [USS] *Maine,* which was sent to the Havana harbor to protect U.S. citizens and property in Cuba. Though the cause of the explosion was never discovered, President McKinley approved a congressional resolution demanding immediate Spanish withdrawal from Cuba. A few days later, Spain declared war.

The congressional resolution stated that the United States was not acting to secure an empire. However, the terms of the Treaty of Paris that officially ended the war required that Spain cede the Philippines, Puerto Rico, and Guam to the United States. For good or ill, the United States had expanded.

1 According to this writer, American involvement in Cuba was most directly triggered by

A   a desire to help and protect the less economically fortunate in this world.

B   a belief that democracy is the only fair form of government.

C   an overriding desire to maintain peace in the Western Hemisphere.

D   a sense of outrage about danger to American lives and property abroad.

2 What is the writer implying by pointing out that the United States gained territory as a result of the war with Spain?

A   The United States did not want an empire.

B   The United States fought the war only to protect the people of Cuba.

C   Spain willingly gave up the Philippines, Puerto Rico, and Guam.

D   The United States wanted to gain territory through the war.

3 To protect the new United States' position in the world, Congress allocated money for building

A   more miles of railroad.

B   the supply of steel and oil.

C   a larger navy.

D   markets for American goods.

World War I

The Great War, later known as World War I, began in Europe in 1914, and a series of alliances brought more and more countries, including eventually the United States, into the conflict.

Directions: Answer the following questions.

4 **Austria-Hungary's declaration of war against Serbia led to a wider conflict because**

A Austria-Hungary's actions angered the United States.

B Serbia had a large colonial empire.

C Serbia was allied with the Allied Powers.

D Franz Ferdinand was beloved throughout Europe.

5 **Austria-Hungary was involved in a wider alliance with**

A Serbia and Russia.

B Germany and the Ottoman Empire.

C Great Britain and France.

D the United States.

Directions: Questions 6 through 9 are based on the information below.

We intend to begin on the first of February unrestricted submarine warfare. We shall endeavor in spite of this to keep the United States of America neutral. In the event of this not succeeding, we make Mexico a proposal of alliance on the following basis: make war together, make peace together, [offer] generous financial support and an understanding on our part that Mexico is to reconquer the lost territory in Texas, New Mexico, and Arizona.

6 **This passage was most likely written by a foreign minister from**

A Russia.

B Germany.

C Great Britain.

D Serbia.

7 **The document's reference to "the lost territory of Mexico" most likely means**

A the people of Texas, New Mexico, and Arizona hoped to be part of Mexico.

B Germany would attack the United States.

C Germany expected Mexico to give up Texas, New Mexico, and Arizona.

D Germany would support Mexico in fighting the United States to regain that territory.

8 **The "unrestricted submarine warfare" described in this passage led to**

A the destruction of Great Britain's navy.

B Russia's withdrawal from the war.

C the creation of the Fourteen Points.

D Congress's declaration of war on Germany.

9 **From the passage, you can infer that**

A Germany shared substantial common interests with Mexico.

B Germany believed that Mexico's military could turn the tide of the war.

C Germany expected the United States to enter the war on the side of the Allies.

D Germany wished to eventually obtain territory itself from the United States.

10 **One of the biggest disadvantages faced by Germany at the beginning of the war was that it**

A was surrounded by neutral nations.

B had to fight a war on two fronts.

C had no access to the Mediterranean Sea.

D was separated from its allies.

11 **According to the map, Germany's initial military focus when war began was toward which nation?**

A France

B Italy

C Russia

D Serbia

12 **What limited the ability of the Central Powers to use the Mediterranean Sea for supply and trade routes?**

A The Russian presence in the Black Sea

B The colonial occupation of most of North Africa by the Allied Powers

C Spain's status as a neutral nation at the western entrance to the Mediterranean Sea

D The extensive territory administered by the Ottoman Empire

13 **How would a map showing Europe after the end of World War I differ from this map to reflect the defeat of Austria-Hungary?**

A The presence of several other nations on the same territory shown here as Austria-Hungary

B The absorption of Serbia into Austria-Hungary

C The disappearance of both Austria and Hungary from the map

D The moving of Austria-Hungary's western border by several hundred miles to the west

After the War

When the war was over, the victorious countries wanted to create a setting in Europe that would ensure peace. President Wilson's plans for world peace were accepted in Europe, but not in the United States.

Directions: Questions 14 through 17 are based on the information below.

We entered this war because violations of right had occurred which touched us to the quick and made the life of our own people impossible unless they were corrected and the world secure once for all against their recurrence. What we demand in this war, therefore, is nothing peculiar to ourselves. It is that the world be made fit and safe to live in; and particularly that it be made safe for every peace-loving nation which, like our own, wishes to live its own life, determine its own institutions, be assured of justice and fair dealing by the other peoples of the world as against force and selfish aggression. All the peoples of the world are in effect partners in this interest, and for our own part we see very clearly that unless justice be done to others it will not be done to us.

—President Woodrow Wilson, January 8, 1918

14 **In this address, President Wilson was most likely expressing his support for the creation of the**

    A League of Nations.

    B Paris Peace Conference.

    C Big Four.

    D Central Powers.

15 **This speech also reflects Wilson's support for the Treaty of Versailles. How did the views of the United States Senate differ from those of Wilson?**

    A Most senators were opposed to the United States' involvement in the war.

    B Most senators believed that the treaty did not do enough to punish Germany.

    C Most senators were opposed to the League of Nations created by the treaty.

    D Most senators refused to recognize the new countries created by the treaty.

16 **What slogan best summarizes Wilson's reasons for going to war?**

    A "Punish Germany"

    B "Secure the World for Ourselves"

    C "Might Makes Right"

    D "Make the World Safe for Democracy"

17 **What does this passage imply about the role of the United States in this conflict?**

    A That the US has no desire to conquer other people or nations

    B That the US will not give up until Germany is under its control

    C That nations opposing the US will face lasting consequences for their actions

    D That the US is an unwilling participant in Europe's conflict

 Test-Taking Tip

When answering multiple choice questions, be sure to read the question closely before you choose your answer.

This lesson will help you understand: the events that led to World War II, the alliances formed during the war, why the US entered the war, and how life in the United States was affected by the war. Use it with Core Lesson 4.2 *World War II* to reinforce and apply your knowledge.

Key Concept

After World War I, three totalitarian governments formed in Europe and began World War II.

The Rise of Dictators

In the years following World War I, totalitarian leaders such as Adolf Hitler and Benito Mussolini were able to seize power by taking advantage of Europe's political and economic instability.

Directions: Questions 1 and 2 are based on the information below.

Excerpt from Adolf Hitler—Speech before the Reichstag January 30, 1937

Four years ago, when I was entrusted with the Chancellorship and therewith the leadership of the nation, I took upon myself the bitter duty of restoring the honor of a nation which for fifteen years had been forced to live as a pariah among the other nations of the world. The internal order which we created among the German people offered the conditions necessary to reorganize the army and also made it possible for me to throw off those shackles which we felt to be the deepest disgrace ever branded on a people. Today I shall bring this whole matter to a close by making the following few declarations:

First: The restoration of Germany's equality of rights was an event that concerned Germany alone. It was not the occasion of taking anything from anybody or causing any suffering to anybody.

Second: I now state here that, in accordance with the restoration of equality of rights, I shall divest the German Railways and the Reichsbank of the forms under which they have hitherto functioned and shall place them absolutely under the sovereign control of the Government of the German Reich.

Third: I hereby declare that the section of the Versailles Treaty which deprived our nation of the rights that it shared on an equal footing with other nations and degraded it to the level of an inferior people found its natural liquidation in virtue of the restoration of equality of status.

Fourth: Above all, I solemnly withdraw the German signature from that declaration which was extracted under duress from a weak government, acting against its better judgment, namely the declaration that Germany was responsible for the war.

1 **Which phrase is an example of bias in Hitler's speech?**

   A "Four years ago, when I was entrusted with the Chancellorship"

   B "those shackles which we felt to be the deepest disgrace ever branded on a people"

   C "place them absolutely under the sovereign control of the Government"

   D "I solemnly withdraw the German signature from that declaration"

2 **To which government is Hitler referring when he uses the phrase, "under duress from a weak government"?**

   A The former German government

   B The government of Great Britain

   C The government of France

   D The former government of Russia

World War II

Provoked by Hitler's conquest of much of Western Europe and by a direct assault by Japanese forces, the United States entered World War II in 1941.

Directions: Questions 3 through 6 are based on the following information.

Soldiers, Sailors and Airmen of the Allied Expeditionary Force! You are about to embark upon the Great Crusade, toward which we have striven these many months. The eyes of the world are upon you. The hopes and prayers of liberty-loving people everywhere march with you. In company with our brave Allies and brothers-in-arms on other Fronts, you will bring about the destruction of the German war machine, the elimination of Nazi tyranny over the oppressed peoples of Europe, and security for ourselves in a free world.

Your task will not be an easy one. Your enemy is well trained, well equipped and battle hardened. He will fight savagely.

But this is the year 1944! Much has happened since the Nazi triumphs of 1940–41. The United Nations have inflicted upon the Germans great defeats, in open battle, man-to-man. Our air offensive has seriously reduced their strength in the air and their capacity to wage war on the ground. Our Home Fronts have given us an overwhelming superiority in weapons and munitions of war, and placed at our disposal great reserves of trained fighting men.

The tide has turned! The free men of the world are marching together to Victory!

I have full confidence in your courage and devotion to duty and skill in battle.

We will accept nothing less than full Victory! Good luck! And let us beseech the blessing of Almighty God upon this great and noble undertaking.

—General Dwight D. Eisenhower, June 2, 1944

3 **Which event is one of the "Nazi triumphs" to which Eisenhower refers in his address?**

A The battle of Stalingrad

B The attack on Pearl Harbor

C The conquest of the Balkans

D The defeat of Mussolini

4 **Based on the information given in this passage, you can conclude that this speech was most likely given immediately before which event?**

A The battle of El Alamein

B The battle of Stalingrad

C The invasion of Japan

D The invasion of France

5 **Which subsequent development proved that the Allies' mission could truly be considered a "Great Crusade"?**

A The discovery of Nazi concentration camps

B The development of the atomic bomb

C The removal of Mussolini from power

D The peace agreements at the Yalta Conference

6 **To whom was Eisenhower giving credit when he said, "Our Home Fronts have given us an overwhelming superiority in weapons and munitions of war . . . "?**

A The people of the United States

B The people of France where D-Day would occur

C The civilian populations of all the Allied countries

D The weapons' manufacturers

President Franklin D. Roosevelt
Excerpt from Pearl Harbor Address to the Nation, December 8, 1941

The attack yesterday on the Hawaiian islands has caused severe damage to American naval and military forces. I regret to tell you that very many American lives have been lost. In addition, American ships have been reported torpedoed on the high seas between San Francisco and Honolulu.

Yesterday, the Japanese government also launched an attack against Malaya.

Last night, Japanese forces attacked Hong Kong.

Last night, Japanese forces attacked Guam.

Last night, Japanese forces attacked the Philippine Islands.

Last night, the Japanese attacked Wake Island.

And this morning, the Japanese attacked Midway Island.

Japan has, therefore, undertaken a surprise offensive extending throughout the Pacific area. The facts of yesterday and today speak for themselves. The people of the United States have already formed their opinions and well understand the implications to the very life and safety of our nation.

As Commander in Chief of the Army and Navy, I have directed that all measures be taken for our defense. But always will our whole nation remember the character of the onslaught against us.

No matter how long it may take us to overcome this premeditated invasion, the American people in their righteous might will win through to absolute victory. . . .

I ask that the Congress declare that since the unprovoked and dastardly attack by Japan on Sunday, December 7th, 1941, a state of war has existed between the United States and the Japanese empire.

7 **What does Roosevelt intend to describe with the phrase, "the facts of yesterday and today"?**

A The lack of American preparation for war in the Pacific

B American neutrality before the war

C Japanese aggression and violence throughout the Pacific

D Plans for American defense

8 **Why was it most important for Roosevelt to use the phrase, "premeditated invasion" in his speech?**

A He wanted to remind people that Pearl Harbor was United States territory.

B He wanted to show that Japan had carefully planned to attack United States territory.

C He wished the American military had been better prepared.

D He hoped Americans would discriminate against Japanese Americans in the United States.

9 **How does the phrase "will win through to absolute victory" foreshadow the American position toward Japan at the end of the war?**

A The United States demanded Japan's unconditional surrender as the only acceptable end to the war with them.

B It alludes to the weaknesses in the Treaty of Versailles at the end of World War I.

C FDR was concerned about how negotiations with the Axis Powers would leave doors open for another war.

D The president wanted to show the world that the United States was not weak and would never negotiate with her enemies.

10 **Which of the following is the best description of the Holocaust?**

A Germany's plan for invading Russia.

B The Nazis' genocide against Jewish people and others

C The policies that allowed Hitler to seize power

D The treatment of Germany after World War I

Americans During the War

On the home front, Americans were unified in their support of the war effort, though many loyal Americans still faced racial and ethnic discrimination.

Directions: Question 11 is based on the information below.

Before the war, college and homeownership were, for the most part, unreachable dreams for the average American. Thanks to the GI Bill, millions who would have flooded the job market instead opted for education. In the peak year of 1947, veterans accounted for 49 percent of college admissions. By the time the original GI Bill ended on July 25, 1956, 7.8 million of 16 million World War II veterans had participated in an education or training program.

Millions also took advantage of the GI Bill's home loan guaranty. From 1944 to 1952, VA backed nearly 2.4 million home loans for World War II veterans.

While veterans embraced the education and home loan benefits, few collected on one of the bill's most controversial provisions—the unemployment pay. Less than 20 percent of funds set aside for this were used.

11 **In addition to preparing more veterans for better jobs through education and training, what other benefit to the economy was a short-term result of the GI Bill?**

   A Veterans were able to delay purchasing new homes while in school.

   B Sending veterans to school boosted the profits of the education industry.

   C Veterans were able to use unemployment pay for college tuition.

   D Sending veterans to school prevented them from overloading the job market after returning home.

 Test-Taking Tip

When you are answering passage-based questions, it is sometimes a good idea to skim the passage first to get an idea of the author's general purpose and tone. Then, read the questions to guide you through a closer reading of the passage.

This lesson will help you understand how communism spread throughout the world, how the United States matured as a world power, and how the world reacted to the Cold War. Use it with Core Lesson 4.3 *The Cold War* to reinforce and apply your knowledge.

Key Concept

After World War II, the United States and the Soviet Union began a Cold War that kept tensions high between the countries.

A Broken Alliance

Following World War II, the United States and the Soviet Union emerged as the world's superpowers, with competing economic and political philosophies.

Directions: Use the map below to help answer questions 1 through 4.

1   **On the map above, the dashed lines represent divisions that had been created as a result of the**

   A   Warsaw Pact.

   B   Treaty of Versailles.

   C   Atlantic Charter.

   D   Yalta Conference.

2   **Which NATO member shared a border with the Soviet Union?**

   A   Norway

   B   Turkey

   C   Austria

   D   Greece

3 Based on the map above, how was Germany different after World War II?

A Germany expanded considerably, gaining new territories from the former Austria-Hungary and from France.

B Germany was divided into zones to be occupied by each of the Allied nations, including an eastern zone that became communist.

C All of Germany was controlled by the Soviet Union and cut off from the rest of Europe.

D Germany was cut up into several smaller nations, each one establishing its own government.

4 Based on the map, how might Denmark's role as a United Nations member be critical to the people of West Germany?

A Denmark's economy depended on goods coming from West Germany.

B The West Germans could count on the Nordic nations of Denmark, Norway, and Sweden for military support.

C The United Nations could depend on Denmark.

D The North Sea is West Germany's only outlet to the Atlantic Ocean, and Denmark would be favorable to their incoming and outgoing shipping.

Directions: Answer the questions below.

5 Why would Berlin as a jointly occupied city be problematic for the western bloc of nations?

A Berlin was deep in the communist controlled area of Germany and could be vulnerable to Soviet tactics.

B Berlin's people would be confused about their government and their future.

C Having Berlin divided into two separate zones created a false sense of calm in the region.

D The western bloc of nations had few concerns about Berlin.

6 The border dividing Europe between western nations and Soviet-influenced nations became known as the

A Demilitarized Zone.

B Western Front.

C Iron Curtain.

D Maginot Line.

7 Despite their postwar differences, leaders of the Soviet Union, Great Britain, and the United States did agree about the

A way the nations between Germany and the Soviet Union should be governed.

B right of people to hold free elections in Eastern Europe.

C formation of a new international organization, the United Nations.

D economic system that would be imposed in the nations of Europe.

8 One feature of the United Nations was the veto power of the five permanent members of the Security Council, including the United States and the Soviet Union. This was a shortcoming because

A both the US and the Soviet Union wished to use force to settle most disputes.

B the US and the Soviet Union refused to share power on the Security Council.

C the Soviet Union demanded a leadership position on the Security Council.

D the US and the Soviet Union disagreed on many important issues.

 Test-Taking Tip

When answering questions involving historic maps, be sure to incorporate your knowledge of the era in question.

The West Responds to Communism

Fearing the spread of communism after World War II, the United States tried to limit the extension of Soviet influence in Europe.

Directions: Questions 9 through 13 are based on the information below.

Soviet power, unlike that of Hitlerite Germany, is neither schematic nor adventuristic. It does not work by fixed plans. It does not take unnecessary risks. Impervious to logic of reason, and it is highly sensitive to logic of force. For this reason it can easily withdraw—and usually does—when strong resistance is encountered at any point. Thus, if the adversary has sufficient force and makes clear his readiness to use it, he rarely has to do so. If situations are properly handled there need be no prestige-engaging showdowns . . .

We must formulate and put forward for other nations a much more positive and constructive picture of [the] sort of world we would like to see than we have put forward in [the] past. It is not enough to urge people to develop political processes similar to our own. Many foreign peoples, in Europe at least, are tired and frightened by experiences of past, and are less interested in abstract freedom than in security. They are seeking guidance rather than responsibilities. We should be better able than Russians to give them this. And, unless we do, Russians certainly will.

—American Diplomat George F. Kennan, 1946

9 The first paragraph of this excerpt expresses a US policy toward combating communism that would later be known as

 A engagement.

 B containment.

 C resistance.

 D aggression.

10 What does Kennan mean by the phrase "highly sensitive to the logic of force"?

 A The Soviet Union would use force against weak countries, regardless of the consequences.

 B The Soviet Union would back down to a country willing to use military force against it.

 C The Soviet Union was prepared to fight the United States.

 D The Soviet Union was very similar to Germany under Hitler.

11 Which international organization carried out Kennan's ideas?

 A The North Atlantic Treaty Organization

 B The Warsaw Pact

 C The United Nations Security Council

 D The Yalta Conference

12 President Truman responded to the Soviet Union's blockade of West Berlin by

 A invading East Germany.

 B withdrawing from the United Nations.

 C building bomb shelters in the United States.

 D airlifting supplies into West Berlin.

13 President Kennedy responded to the Soviet Union's demand that West Berlin be joined with East Berlin under a Communist government by

 A building the Berlin Wall.

 B sending troops to West Berlin.

 C signing a peace treaty with East Germany.

 D agreeing to the demands.

Communism Outside Europe

As the inauguration of President John Kennedy signaled a new era in American politics, the United States faced new threats in the form of communist governments in Cuba and in Southeast Asia.

Directions: Questions 14 and 15 are based on the information below.

To those peoples in the huts and villages across the globe struggling to break the bonds of mass misery, we pledge our best efforts to help them help themselves, for whatever period is required—not because the Communists may be doing it, not because we seek their votes, but because it is right. If a free society cannot help the many who are poor, it cannot save the few who are rich.

To our sister republics south of our border, we offer a special pledge—to convert our good words into good deeds—in a new alliance for progress—to assist free men and free governments in casting off the chains of poverty. But this peaceful revolution of hope cannot become the prey of hostile powers. Let all our neighbors know that we shall join with them to oppose aggression or subversion anywhere in the Americas. And let every other power know that this Hemisphere intends to remain the master of its own house.

—President John F. Kennedy, Inaugural Address

14 One reason Kennedy might have been especially concerned about the plight of "our sister republics south of our border" was that thousands of refugees were fleeing Cuba to the United States to escape

A extreme poverty and slavery.

B the rule of the Catholic church.

C the communist government of Fidel Castro.

D Soviet nuclear missiles.

15 President Kennedy demonstrated that he was willing "to oppose aggression or subversion anywhere in the Americas" by

A setting up a naval blockade around Cuba.

B testing nuclear weapons in the Caribbean.

C disconnecting the hotline to the Soviet Union.

D deploying nuclear missiles to Turkey.

Directions: Answer the questions below.

16 President Johnson carried on Kennedy's foreign policy by

A granting independence to India and Pakistan.

B opposing colonial rule in Africa.

C increasing the number of troops in Vietnam.

D holding peace talks with Nikita Khrushchev.

17 What is the most likely reason that France opposed decolonization in French Indochina (Vietnam)?

A France wanted to extend its colonial empire throughout Southeast Asia.

B France was opposed to the communist government of Ho Chi Minh.

C France wanted the United States to take control of Vietnam.

D France was against the formation of independent nations.

This lesson will help you understand the achievements and failures of the Johnson and Nixon administrations and their connections to the collapse of communism. Use it with Core Lesson 4.4 *Societal Changes* to reinforce and apply your knowledge.

Key Concept

During the second half of the twentieth century, the United States struggled with scandals at home and communism abroad.

The Great Society

The presidency of Lyndon Johnson was defined by Great Society programs and the Vietnam War.

Directions: Questions 1 through 3 are based on the information below.

The Great Society rests on abundance and liberty for all. It demands an end to poverty and racial injustice, to which we are totally committed in our time. But that is just the beginning. The Great Society is a place where every child can find knowledge to enrich his mind and to enlarge his talents. It is a place where leisure is a welcome chance to build and reflect, not a feared cause of boredom and restlessness. It is a place where the city of man serves not only the needs of the body and the demands of commerce but the desire for beauty and the hunger for community. It is a place where man can renew contact with nature. It is a place which honors creation for its own sake and for what it adds to the understanding of the race. It is a place where men are more concerned with the quality of their goals than the quantity of their goods. But most of all, the Great Society is not a safe harbor, a resting place, a final objective, a finished work. It is a challenge constantly renewed, beckoning us toward a destiny where the meaning of our lives matches the marvelous products of our labor.

—President Lyndon B. Johnson, Great Society Speech, 1964

1 **According to the passage, which of these is one major focus of the Great Society?**

  A Greater production of goods

  B Increased industrial production

  C Environmental enrichment

  D Greater retirement options

2 **The new agency created in 1964 to manage programs aiding the poor was called the**

  A Department of the Interior.

  B Office of Economic Opportunity.

  C Peace Corps.

  D Department of Housing and Urban Development.

3 **If Great Society programs were entirely successful, according to Johnson, what would be one likely result?**

  A People of all races would be assured equal rights.

  B All adult citizens would have more leisure time.

  C Laws would prevent any adverse effects on the environment.

  D All citizens could buy the products they wanted.

Directions: Answer the questions below.

4 Under the Great Society, a person who wanted to report charges of discrimination in the workplace could appeal to

    A VISTA.

    B the Community Action Program.

    C the EEOC.

    D the Voting Rights Act.

5 Which Great Society program supported democratic principles by giving people the opportunity to be more active in how government affected their neighborhoods?

    A VISTA

    B Community Action Program

    C EEOC

    D the Voting Rights Act

The Nixon Administration

President Richard Nixon ended the Vietnam War and introduced policies of New Federalism, but was eventually forced to resign as a result of the Watergate scandal.

Directions: Answer the questions below.

6 Richard Nixon won the 1968 presidential election following what event earlier that year?

    A The announcement by President Johnson that he would not seek election to another term

    B A delay in the presidential primaries due to the Vietnam War

    C The defeat of President Johnson in the Democratic Party primary election

    D The Watergate scandal

7 What was the purpose of the "New Federalism" of the Nixon Administration?

    A To end the Vietnam War by defeating Vietnam

    B To extend the Great Society by beginning more social programs

    C To return power and tax money to the states

    D To help federal prosecutors solve the Watergate affair

8 The Vietnam War ended during the Nixon presidency with what event?

    A The reunification of North and South Vietnam

    B The surrender of South Vietnam to North Vietnam

    C The occupation of North Vietnam by the United States

    D The signing of the Paris Peace Accords

9 President Nixon's opposition to President Johnson's Great Society programs was based on the belief that

    A assistance to the poor was never the responsibility of the federal government.

    B the government should be more focused on the Vietnam War.

    C such programs gave the federal government too much control over people's lives.

    D the government did not have the Constitutional power to enact such programs.

Since March, when I first learned that the Watergate affair might in fact be far more serious than I had been led to believe, it has claimed far too much of my time and my attention. Whatever may now transpire in the case, whatever the actions of the grand jury, whatever the outcome of any eventual trials, I must now turn my full attention—and I shall do so—once again to the larger duties of this office. I owe it to this great office that I hold, and I owe it to you—to my country…Tomorrow, for example, Chancellor Brandt of West Germany will visit the White House for talks that are a vital element of "The Year of Europe," as 1973 has been called. We are already preparing for the next Soviet-American summit meeting later this year.

This is also a year in which we are seeking to negotiate a mutual and balanced reduction of armed forces in Europe, which will reduce our defense budget and allow us to have funds for other purposes at home so desperately needed. It is the year when the United States and Soviet negotiators will seek to work out the second and even more important round of our talks on limiting nuclear arms and of reducing the danger of a nuclear war that would destroy civilization as we know it. It is a year in which we confront the difficult tasks of maintaining peace in Southeast Asia and in the potentially explosive Middle East.

—President Richard M. Nixon, First Watergate Speech, 1973

10 **Of all of the issues mentions in President Nixon's speech, which of the following contributed most to his resignation?**

    A Terrorism in the Middle East

    B Conflict in Southeast Asia

    C Nuclear arms control

    D The Watergate affair

11 **At the time Nixon gave this speech, which of the following appears to be true?**

    A The House Judiciary Committee had voted for Nixon's impeachment.

    B Transcripts of White House tapes had been provided to the Congress.

    C Five men who had broken into Democratic offices had been arrested.

    D Nixon had decided to resign from the presidency.

12 **According to the speech, Nixon was focused on which of these instead of the Watergate affair?**

    A Ending communism in the Soviet Union

    B Reducing taxes for working US families

    C Increasing US military presence overseas

    D Reducing the worldwide nuclear threat

13 **What is most likely the main purpose of this speech?**

    A To promote "The Year of Europe"

    B To redirect the nation's attention away from the Watergate affair

    C To convince the public that the president is focused on international issues

    D To prove that the Watergate affair was not serious

 Test-Taking Tip

When test questions are preceded by a written passage, read the questions first and then look for the answers as you read the passage.

Communism in China and the Soviet Union

Improvements in relations between the United States and communist countries and societal changes over many decades eventually led to the birth of democracy in Eastern European nations and the dissolution of the Soviet Union.

Directions: Answer the following questions.

14 **Relations between China and the Soviet Union during the Cold War were**

   A close because of their shared status as large communist nations.

   B strained because of their conflict during World War II.

   C close because of their mutual suspicion of the United States.

   D strained because of their large shared border and different interpretations of communism.

15 **In what year did Nixon open diplomatic relations with China and sign an arms agreement with the Soviet Union?**

   A 1971

   B 1972

   C 1985

   D 1989

16 **President Nixon believed that improved relations with China would**

   A force the Soviet Union to attack China.

   B make the Soviet Union abandon communism.

   C convince the Soviet Union to stop building nuclear weapons.

   D limit the Soviet Union's international influence.

17 **Nixon's visit to China started diplomatic communications that had previously been cut off during which decade?**

   A 1930s

   B 1940s

   C 1950s

   D 1960s

18 **The Strategic Arms Limitation Treaty (SALT), signed in 1972, served what purpose?**

   A To freeze the production of long-range offensive missiles

   B To remove restrictions on borders in Eastern Europe

   C To reduce the size of United States and Soviet armies stationed in Europe

   D To eliminate nuclear weapons worldwide

19 **Communism came to an end in the Soviet Union following what development?**

   A The surrender of Soviet troops to NATO forces

   B Democratic reforms begun by Soviet leader Mikhail Gorbachev

   C The collapse of the Soviet economy

   D A negotiated truce between Soviet leaders and democratic activists in the USSR

This lesson will help you understand how US government policies changed after the terrorist attacks on September 11, 2001. Use it with Core Lesson 4.5 *Foreign Policy in the 21ˢᵗ Century* to reinforce and apply your knowledge.

Key Concept

In the first decade of the twenty-first century, the United States experienced a terrorist attack that reshaped government and policies.

Terrorism in the United States

Terrorist attacks on the United States in the 1990s and early 2000s were linked to Osama bin Laden and the Middle-Eastern terrorist group known as al-Qaeda.

Directions: Study the time line below. Then answer questions 1 and 2.

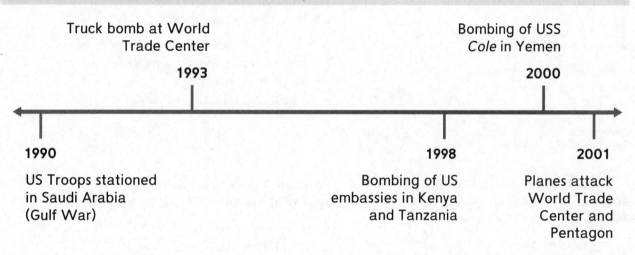

1 **Which event on the time line led Osama bin Laden to attempt to force Westerners out of the Middle East?**

   A Bombing of US embassies in Kenya and Tanzania

   B Bombing of USS *Cole* in Yemen

   C Truck bomb at World Trade Center

   D US troops stationed in Saudi Arabia (Gulf War)

2 **Which event was immediately before the terrorist attacks on the World Trade Center and Pentagon?**

   A Bombing of US embassies in Kenya and Tanzania

   B Bombing of USS *Cole* in Yemen

   C Truck bomb at World Trade Center

   D US Troops stationed in Saudi Arabia (Gulf War)

Directions: Questions 3 and 4 are based on the following information.

Today, our fellow citizens, our way of life, our very freedom came under attack in a series of deliberate and deadly terrorist acts. The victims were in airplanes or in their offices: secretaries, business men and women, military and federal workers, moms and dads, friends and neighbors. Thousands of lives were suddenly ended by evil, despicable acts of terror. The pictures of airplanes flying into buildings, fires burning, huge—huge structures collapsing have filled us with disbelief, terrible sadness, and a quiet, unyielding anger. These acts of mass murder were intended to frighten our nation into chaos and retreat. But they have failed. Our country is strong.

A great people has been moved to defend a great nation. Terrorist attacks can shake the foundations of our biggest buildings, but they cannot touch the foundation of America. These acts shatter steel, but they cannot dent the steel of American resolve. America was targeted for attack because we're the brightest beacon for freedom and opportunity in the world. And no one will keep that light from shining. Today, our nation saw evil—the very worst of human nature—and we responded with the best of America. With the daring of our rescue workers, with the caring for strangers and neighbors who came to give blood and help in any way they could.

—President George W. Bush, Address to the Nation, September 11, 2001

3 According to President Bush, terrorists attacked the United States on September 11 because they were resentful of its

  A great wealth.

  B ethnic diversity.

  C military power.

  D democratic system.

4 According to President Bush, the attack on September 11, 2001, was a terrorist attack. This type of attack is characterized by which of these strategies?

  A use of propaganda to incite violence

  B use of force to overthrow governments

  C use of violence to frighten opponents

  D use of demonstrations to protest policies

Directions: Answer the following questions.

5 Which of the following would members of al-Qaeda most likely use to justify their attacks against American targets?

  A Islamic principles should be used to run countries with large Muslim populations.

  B Fundamentalism can be dangerous, but only when it is practiced in Western nations.

  C Westerners are welcome in the Middle East, as long as they remain politically neutral.

  D Only traditional tools and technologies can be used to halt the spread of Western values.

6 Which of the following events was a direct result of the attack on the World Trade Center and Pentagon?

  A Osama bin Laden was assassinated.

  B Weapons of mass destruction were found in Iraq.

  C The Taliban government was overthrown in Afghanistan.

  D Saddam Hussein was convicted of crimes against humanity.

7 President Bush's first response to the attacks of September 11, 2001, was to

  A assassinate Osama bin Laden.

  B invade Iraq.

  C put Saddam Hussein on trial.

  D launch a war against Afghanistan.

8 On September 11, 2001, three of the four hijacked planes reached the hijackers' targets. Where did the fourth plane crash due to its passengers' resistance?

  A Maryland

  B Connecticut

  C Pennsylvania

  D West Virginia

The Global War on Terror

In response to the terrorist attacks of 9/11, the United States launched an anti-terrorism campaign that has become known as the global war on terror.

Directions: Study the time line below. Then answer questions 9 and 10.

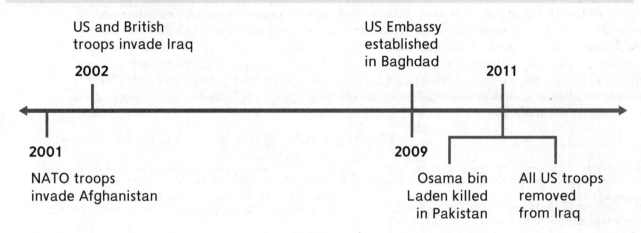

9 This time line illustrates the effect that the terrorist attacks of 9/11 had on US

   A immigration policy.

   B domestic policy.

   C economic policy.

   D foreign policy.

10 Based on the time line, what is the <u>best</u> description of the US global war on terror?

   A Iraq and Afghanistan have been the main focus of the global war on terror.

   B The global war on terror was won in 2011.

   C Pakistan replaced Iraq as a focal point of the US global war on terror.

   D Afghanistan is no longer a focus of the US global war on terror.

Directions: Answer the questions below.

11 Following the September 11, 2001 attacks, what action was taken for the first time in history?

   A Unilateral US military action against another nation

   B US military action in the Eastern Hemisphere

   C Cooperation between NATO forces and former Warsaw Pact nations

   D The invoking by NATO of Article 5 of the Washington Treaty

12 The Iraqi weapons of mass destruction, which were the justification for US military action against Iraq in 2003,

   A included biological warfare agents.

   B were never found.

   C had been supplied by North Korea.

   D had been previously used against Israel.

✔ Test-Taking Tip

When you are drawing a conclusion about a series of events on a time line, try to identify what the different events have in common.

Directions: Questions 13 through 16 are based on the following information.

(1) North Korea is a regime arming with missiles and weapons of mass destruction, while starving its citizens. (2) Iran aggressively pursues these weapons and exports terror, while an unelected few repress the Iranian people's hope for freedom. (3) Iraq continues to flaunt its hostility toward America and to support terror. (4) The Iraqi regime has plotted to develop anthrax and nerve gas and nuclear weapons for over a decade. (5) This is a regime that has already used poison gas to murder thousands of its own citizens, leaving the bodies of mothers huddled over their dead children. (6) This is a regime that agreed to international inspections then kicked out the inspectors. (7) This is a regime that has something to hide from the civilized world. (8) States like these, and their terrorist allies, constitute an axis of evil, arming to threaten the peace of the world. (9) By seeking weapons of mass destruction, these regimes pose a grave and growing danger. (10) They could provide these arms to terrorists, giving them the means to match their hatred. (11) They could attack our allies or attempt to blackmail the United States. (12) In any of these cases, the price of indifference would be catastrophic.

—President George W. Bush, State of the Union Address, 2002

13 President Bush most likely gave this speech to support the

   A passage of the Patriot Act.

   B creation of the Department of Homeland Security.

   C invasion of Iraq.

   D assassination of Osama bin Laden.

14 Which sentence includes language that is meant to evoke an emotional response in those hearing the speech?

   A Sentence 3

   B Sentence 5

   C Sentence 7

   D Sentence 9

15 Although President Bush's speech mentions several nations, the United States focused its military actions on

   A Pakistan.

   B Iran.

   C North Korea.

   D Iraq.

16 According to President Bush's speech, the nations discussed in this speech "constitute an axis of evil" because they

   A have mistreated international weapons inspectors.

   B are developing weapons of mass destruction.

   C are wasting resources that could benefit their people.

   D have directly attacked the United States.

Directions: Answer the questions below.

17 The US invasion of Iraq in 2003 was carried out with the cooperation of

   A NATO

   B Great Britain

   C France

   D The United Nations

18 The war to overthrow Saddam Hussein in Iraq

   A began with eighteen months of heavy fighting, followed by an end to hostilities.

   B began with the immediate surrender of Iraqi forces, followed by several weeks of fighting among insurgent groups.

   C began with six months of heavy fighting, followed by an end to hostilities.

   D began with under a month of heavy fighting, followed by several years of fighting among insurgent groups.

This lesson will help you understand the nature of markets and how competition and monopolies affect the economy. Use it with Core Lesson 5.1 *Markets, Competition, and Monopolies* to reinforce and apply your knowledge.

Key Concept

Buyers and sellers exchange goods and services in a market. Monopoly occurs when a business in a market has no competition. With many businesses in a market, competition can thrive.

Markets

The economy is made of markets in which people and businesses exchange goods and services.

Directions: Answer the following questions.

1 Based on the Key Concept above, what is the best definition of "market"?

  A A type of work that meets a particular need

  B A relationship that makes buying and selling easier

  C A process of offering price and quality to gain business

  D A place where services but not goods are provided

2 Which of the following would be considered a market?

  A A private golf course

  B A forest preserve

  C A classroom

  D An aircraft carrier

3 In a market economy, business owners provide

  A labor and receive wages.

  B resources and receive payments for providing those payments.

  C goods and services and receive income for providing those goods and services.

  D money and receive goods and services for that money.

4 Which outcome is most likely when a soft drink becomes very popular?

  A The manufacturer will cut the price to make the drink more popular.

  B The manufacturer might increase the price of the drink.

  C The manufacturer's cost of making the drink rises.

  D The manufacturer keeps the price the same.

5 Who is most likely to be at a disadvantage in a market economy when resources are scarce?

  A Business owners who buy the resources

  B Owners of resources who provide materials for production

  C Workers who use resources to make goods or provide services

  D People who do not have enough money to pay for resources

6 Which of the following companies is most likely to offer goods and services?

  A Publisher

  B Auto repair shop

  C Doctor's office

  D Bookstore

Competition

When there is competition in the market, buyers have more choices and more control over how much they have to pay for the goods and services they buy.

Directions: Use the chart below to help answer questions 7 and 8.

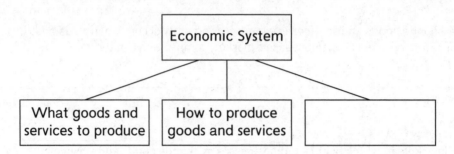

7 **Look at the above diagram. Which of the following statements would fit in the third box?**

A Why to produce them

B How much to sell them for

C Where to get the resources

D For whom to produce them

8 **To ensure a competitive economic system, a government with a market economy**

A sets maximum and minimum prices for goods and services.

B keeps producers from agreeing to set prices or limit supplies.

C limits the amount of information available to buyers and sellers.

D does not allow buyers and sellers to leave the market at will.

Directions: Questions 9 and 10 are based on the following information.

It is not from the benevolence of the butcher, the brewer, or the baker that we expect our dinner, but from their regard to their own interest. We address ourselves, not to their humanity but to their self-love. . . . Give me what I want, and you shall have this which you want, is the meaning of every such offer; and it is the manner that we obtain from one another the far greater part of those good offices which we stand in need of.

—Adam Smith,
The Wealth of Nations, 1776

9 **According to Smith's idea of how buyers are motivated, what do "the butcher, the brewer, or the baker" most likely want in exchange for their products?**

A Respect

B Money

C Self-love

D Interest

10 **If we need meat for dinner but cannot afford to pay for it, why is it futile to depend on the butcher to provide it for free?**

A The butcher is motivated by generosity.

B The butcher wants to be generous but can't afford to be.

C The butcher must compete with the brewer and the baker.

D The butcher is motivated only by self-interest.

Directions: Use the advertising copy below to answer questions 11 and 12.

Ben and Sue's Restaurant, in business for 30 years, features all original recipes from Chef Janison; NOW we are hosting live entertainment every Thursday through Saturday nights; all local musicians. Come and enjoy the atmosphere, and bring a few friends.

11 The ad is an example of how a business can engage in which of the following?

   A Specialization

   B Psychological advertising

   C Non-price competition

   D Goods

12 If Ben and Sue's restaurant closes, and other restaurants see no change in their business, that is a sign of

   A a perfectly competitive market.

   B a monopoly.

   C a declining market.

   D an unbalanced market.

Monopolies

The government has enacted several laws to prevent monopolies from forming. There are several kinds of monopolies. Companies often spend large amounts of money in research to develop new products for which they can acquire patents. This gives them the exclusive right to sell the product for many years.

Directions: Answer the following questions.

13 Which of the following is the most likely behavior of a company that is a monopoly?

   A It changes its prices based on buyers' desires.

   B It freely shares information about its products.

   C It produces a unique product.

   D It invests a lot of money on advertising.

14 A patent is to a new product, as what is to a work of art?

   A Market

   B Competition

   C Monopoly

   D Copyright

15 Which of the following is another term for monopoly?

   A Competitor

   B Marketplace

   C Capital

   D Trust

16 Which of these market characteristics pertain to a monopoly?

   A Many buyers and sellers in the market each account for only a small amount of the market output.

   B A company produces a unique product for which there is no easy substitute.

   C A company has no control over price.

   D Buyers have all of the information they need about price, quality, and product availability.

✔ **Test-Taking Tip**

In multiple-choice questions, if two answers contradict each other, one of them is likely to be the correct answer.

Directions: Use the chart below to answer questions 16 and 17.

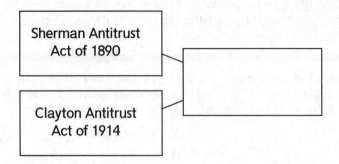

Sherman Antitrust
Act of 1890

Clayton Antitrust
Act of 1914

17 **Look at the diagram above. What was the purpose of these two acts?**

A   To prevent monopolies

B   To encourage research and development

C   To protect patents

D   To interfere with markets

18 **The Sherman and Clayton Antitrust Acts are examples of government action designed to**

A   increase the profits of large corporations.

B   keep markets competitive.

C   limit trade.

D   set fair prices for consumers.

Directions: Answer the following questions.

19 **How is a technological monopoly formed?**

A   When a company controls the sale of technology products, such as computers

B   When a company makes a unique product that is developed with technology, sells it, and protects it with a patent

C   When a company makes a product that qualifies for patent and copyright protection

D   When a company qualifies for antitrust protection

20 **Because it does not have to worry about what rivals are charging, a monopoly has a great deal of control over**

A   price.

B   competitors.

C   demand.

D   regulations.

21 **A monopoly generally produces something that**

A   has recently been introduced to the market.

B   is manufactured by no more than two companies.

C   is closely regulated by the government.

D   has no other substitute available.

22 **Like perfect competition, pure monopoly**

A   returns periodically in a market economy.

B   is a signal of an economic slowdown.

C   only exists in theory.

D   requires cooperation between industries.

This lesson will help you understand the four factors of production that make all markets work. Use it with Core Lesson 5.2 *Factors of Production* to reinforce and apply your knowledge.

Key Concept

The factors of production, which include natural resources, labor, capital, and entrepreneurship, are used to produce goods and services.

Scarcity and Choice

Everyone has needs and wants—things we must have to survive and other things that we would enjoy having. However, we have a limited amount of money to spend on both. How do we choose?

Directions: Answer the following questions.

1 Scarcity is usually understood as the rarity or short supply of something. In economics, however, scarcity depends on two criteria. What are they?

A Ease of production and price

B Natural resources and cost of goods

C Less supply than demand, and the product has value

D More supply than demand, and the product has value

2 Relative scarcity occurs when

A the supply of a product drops dramatically.

B the supply of a product stays the same, but a higher value is attached to the product.

C the supply of a product rises more quickly than the demand for that product.

D the supply and demand for a product stay relatively equal.

3 A video game that sold for $49.95 when it came out now sells for $9.95 two years later. What most likely caused this drop in price?

A The product was poorly marketed.

B Production of the game exceeded the demand.

C High demand for the product drove prices down.

D The opportunity cost was too high.

4 Opportunity cost refers to the cost of

A the next-best alternative.

B the alternative chosen.

C the resources used to produce an item or service.

D the resources used by a competitor.

⚡ Test-Taking Tip

When you are answering multiple-choice questions, use the process of elimination. That is, first eliminate all answers you know are definitely incorrect. Then analyze the remaining options to determine the correct answer.

Directions: Questions 5 and 6 are based on the following information.

Your cell phone has stopped working, and you need to buy a new one. Two models offer the same benefits, but one costs $50.00 more than the other. You wanted to use that $50.00 to take a friend to her favorite restaurant for her birthday. After reading the reviews of both phone models, you choose the more expensive one and decide to make a nice dinner at home for your friend.

5 What is the opportunity cost of this decision?

  A Taking your friend to a restaurant

  B Getting a better phone for more money

  C Making her birthday dinner at home

  D Spending $50.00 more than you wanted to spend

6 In the scenario above, you based your decision on

  A need.

  B phone model.

  C want.

  D opportunity cost.

Natural and Human Resources

Two of the four factors of production involve natural resources and human resources.

Directions: Answer the following questions.

7 Which of the following factors of production is the most difficult for business owners to control?

  A Human resources

  B Natural resources

  C Capital resources

  D Entrepreneurship

8 Which of the following is a nonrenewable resource?

  A The land on which wheat is grown

  B Wheat grown on farmland

  C The grain produced from the wheat

  D Trees that are grown to shade the house of the wheat farmer

9 Which factor of production is most dependent on human creativity?

  A Human resources

  B Natural resources

  C Capital resources

  D Entrepreneurship

10 The supply of nonrenewable resources

  A must be replenished regularly.

  B cannot be easily replenished.

  C is not limited.

  D is no longer widely used in most markets.

Directions: Questions 11 through 14 are based on the following information.

In the 1830s, Samuel Colt invented the Colt revolver. This gun could be fired six times without reloading. Many people claim that it helped the United States settle the West. Colt had a plan for manufacturing his guns. He explained his idea in a letter to his father:

"The first workman would receive two or three of the most important parts, and would affix these together and pass them on to the next who would do the same, and so on until the complete [revolver] is put together. It would then be inspected and given the finishing touches by experts and each [gun] would be exactly alike and all of its parts would be the same. The workmen, by constant practice in a single operation, would become highly skilled and at the same time very quick and expert at their particular task. So you have better guns and more of them for less money than if you hire men and have each one make the entire [revolver]."

—Quoted in *Yankee Arms Maker: The Incredible Career of Samuel Colt,* by Jack Rohan (Harper & Bros., 1935).

11 **Which factor of production was the main focus of Samuel Colt's idea?**

  A Natural resources

  B Human resources

  C Relative scarcity

  D Supply and demand

12 **Why did he think this method would improve productivity?**

  A The workers would take more pride in their work.

  B The value of the product would rise in the market.

  C The quality and the speed of production would increase.

  D The cost of production would be less dependent on natural resources.

13 **How would employment be affected by this method?**

  A More products could be produced by fewer workers.

  B More workers would be needed to meet demand.

  C Experienced workers could demand higher wages for their work.

  D A shortage of workers would be an ongoing concern.

14 **What is one potential drawback of Colt's system?**

  A The monotony of a worker's performing the same task repeatedly

  B The increasing number of tasks performed by each worker

  C Workers' increased reliance on machinery

  D Less predictability in the speed of production

Capital and Entrepreneurship

When you combine capital resources with natural resources and labor, more goods and services can be produced.

Directions: Answer the following questions.

15 Through which of the following factors of production did Henry Ford improve productivity of Ford Motor Company?

A Human resources

B Natural resources

C Capital resources

D Entrepreneurship

16 To produce goods and services, what must be applied to natural resources and human resources?

A Capital

B Entrepreneurship

C Technology

D Tools

Directions: Questions 17 through 19 are based on the following information.

In 1902 Hershey began producing its famous "KISSES®" candy pieces." Each individual KISS® was wrapped by hand. Then in 1921, an invention called a channel wrapper made this labor-intensive part of the process much faster. At the same time, the famous strip of paper—the "plume"—was added. During World War II, the making of KISSES® was put on hold because the silver foil (aluminum) was rationed. Today more than 1,300 KISSES® per minute are produced.

17 The channel wrapper introduced by the Hershey company is an example of which factor of production?

A Natural resources

B Capital resources

C Labor

D Production quality

18 The introduction of the channel wrapper by the Hershey company most directly affected which factor of production?

A Natural resources

B Capital resources

C Labor

D Production quality

19 Manufacturers such as Hershey best handle rationing—the regulation of quantities and kinds of goods bought, sold, and traded—by

A reducing the labor force.

B stopping production until the rationing is lifted.

C increasing their capital costs by adding new machinery.

D finding alternative natural resources that work well.

This lesson will help you understand how businesses can increase profits and productivity. Use it with Core Lesson 5.3 *Profits and Productivity* to reinforce and apply your knowledge.

Key Concept

The possibility of increased profits is an incentive for business owners to take risks, expand, and try various strategies that will increase productivity.

Risks and Profits

Starting a new business is risky, but entrepreneurs and workers are willing to take risks to make a profit.

Directions: Use the graph below to help answer questions 1 through 4.

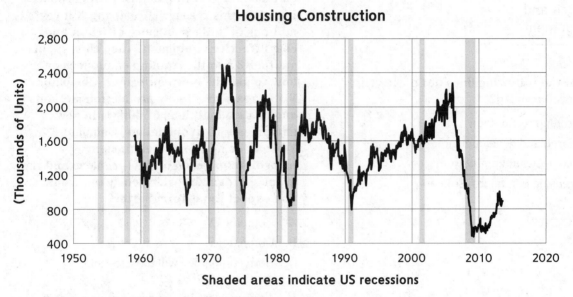

Housing Construction

Shaded areas indicate US recessions

Source: http://research.stlouisfed.org/fred2/graph/?s%5b1%5d%5bid%5d=HOUST

1   **Which period between recessions showed the least fluctuation in housing construction?**

   A   The 1960s

   B   The second half of the 1970s

   C   The mid-to-late 1980s

   D   The 1990s

2   **In which decade would investing in housing at the beginning of the decade have resulted in the greatest profit by the end of that decade?**

   A   1970s

   B   1980s

   C   1990s

   D   2000s

3   **According to the graph, home builders took the most risks to start new housing units**

   A   between 1960 and 1970.

   B   between 1970 and 1975.

   C   in 1990.

   D   around 2005.

4   **Based on the data in this graph, what is the greatest risk for a homebuilder?**

   A   Threat of a recession

   B   Rising cost of materials

   C   Declining number of houses on the market

   D   Period of time that it takes to construct a house

Productivity and Profits

One way that businesses increase profits is through productivity.

Directions: Use the graphic organizer below to help answer questions 5 through 7.

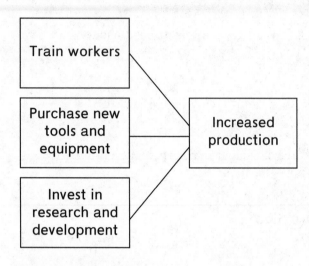

5 **Which of the following does not positively impact productivity?**

   A Upgrading technology

   B Research and development

   C Employee training programs

   D Decreasing capital investments

6 **What is the opportunity cost associated with the graphic shown here?**

   A An increase in available capital

   B A decrease in goods and an increase in services produced

   C A temporary increase in output

   D A temporary drop in current production

7 **Company X researched new production methods for creating labels for its products. Based on this research, Company X invested millions of dollars on more efficient and cost effective equipment. They then spent another 2 months training employees on how to use the new equipment. Company Y also researched new production methods and invested millions of dollars in new equipment. To avoid delays, Company Y began using the new equipment immediately. Based on this scenario and the graphic organizer, which company would you expect to perform better?**

   A Company X

   B Company Y

   C Both companies will have the same results.

   D Neither company will see return on their investment in equipment.

 Test-Taking Tip

To answer questions related to a chart or graph, first carefully read the title. Then identify the units that are used in plotting the chart or graph. Finally, determine the trend, conditions, or measurements that the chart or graph is attempting to show.

Global Top Ten Firms Spending (in billions) on Research and Development in a Recent Year		
Roche Holding	global health care	$9.1
Microsoft	software, electronics	$9
Nokia	telecommunications	$8.2
Toyota	automobiles	$7.8
Pfizer	pharmaceuticals	$7.7
Novartis	pharmaceuticals	$7.5
Johnson & Johnson	pharmaceutical	$7
Sanofi	Aventis pharmaceuticals	$6.3
Glaxo Smith Kline	pharmaceuticals	$6.2
Samsung	electronics	$6

Source: *The Christian Science Monitor*

8 According to the chart, which group of companies spends the most on research and development?

A Automobiles

B Electronics

C Global healthcare

D Pharmaceuticals

9 Which aspect of business might justify large expenses for research and development in these or any companies?

A Rising costs

B Potential increased earnings

C The lack of competition

D The number of people in the market

Directions: Answer the following questions.

10 Which of the following describes an increase in productivity?

A Less input produces less output.

B More input produces less output.

C Less or equal input produces more output.

D More input produces more output.

11 Which of the following would boost a company's current level of productivity?

A A labor shortage

B Research and development

C Increasing capital and human and natural resources

D Decreasing capital and human and natural resources

12 Buildings and equipment owned by bicycle manufacturer are part of that company's

A capital.

B opportunity cost.

C natural resources.

D potential value.

13 Mass production was first made possible by

A the minimum wage.

B the assembly line.

C capital.

D depreciation.

Incentives and Risk-Taking

Individuals and businesses are more willing to take risks and invest in their new products if they are encouraged with incentives.

Directions: Answer the following questions.

14 What limits the value of entrepreneurship in a traditional economy?

  A Entrepreneurship cannot be purchased in a traditional economy.

  B Workers freely acquire new jobs and new skills in a traditional economy.

  C There is a high level of competition in a traditional economy.

  D People have no incentive to try new ideas or to invent new products.

15 In the United States, the government has the right to take away a person's property if the government

  A owns the property.

  B arrests the property owner.

  C takes the property by force.

  D pays the owner for the property.

16 In a market economy, the value of natural resources, human resources, and capital resources increases because

  A each of these resources can be bought or sold.

  B a market economy uses business strategies to increase those resources.

  C a market economy has incentives to achieve profit.

  D the government offers those resources for sale.

17 Why is there often a sharp increase in economic growth in a country with a command economy that removes its restrictions and allows free market incentives to take place?

  A The government in a country with a command economy forces people to work harder.

  B Workers in a command economy cannot adapt to new freedoms because they are used to getting paid no matter how productive they are.

  C Increased economic freedom and opportunity give people incentives to produce more goods and services.

  D The government in a country with a command economy is more adaptable to free market conditions.

18 Which of the following is an incentive that companies can offer to their employees?

  A Capital resources

  B Guaranteed wages

  C Business strategies

  D Performance bonuses

19 Which type of economy is no longer found on a national scale in any country?

  A Mixed

  B Command

  C Planned

  D Traditional

This lesson will help you understand how and why businesses decide what they are going to produce by looking at what other companies produce. Use it with Core Lesson 5.4 *Specialization and Comparative Advantage* to reinforce and apply your knowledge.

Key Concept

Specialization increases productivity and provides businesses with a comparative advantage, but it also leads to interdependence.

Specialization

Specialization is when a company decides to focus on making only a few goods or providing a limited number of services. This helps the company become more profitable because it finds ways to be highly efficient.

Directions: Answer the following questions.

1 **Consider this chart.**

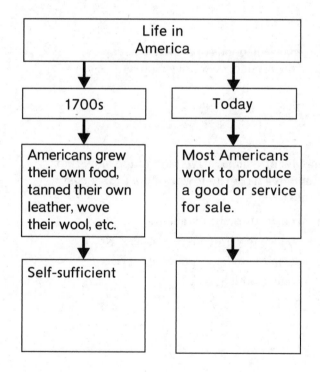

Which word best fits the empty box in the chart?

A Opportunity cost

B Comparative advantage

C Absolute advantage

D Specialization

2 **Which of the following describes the connection between comparative advantage and opportunity cost?**

A A low comparative advantage is a result of low opportunity cost.

B A high comparative advantage is a result of high opportunity cost.

C A high comparative advantage is a result of low opportunity cost.

D Comparative advantage and opportunity cost are the same.

3 **An absolute advantage is the ability to produce a product or service using**

A fewer resources than other producers.

B more resources than other producers.

C fewer human resources than other producers.

D more specialized resources than other producers.

Lesson 5.4 Specialization and Comparative Advantage

Directions: Questions 4 and 5 are based on the following information.

With more than a century of growing potatoes, Idaho has produced more than any other state every year since 1957, producing around 30 percent of the US fall production per year. Bingham County produces almost more potatoes than the entire state of Maine. Potatoes contribute more than $2 billion, or approximately 15%, of Idaho's gross state product.

—Idaho State Department of Education

4 **Which of the following statements best describes Idaho's market position in potatoes?**

A Idaho has a higher comparative advantage in growing potatoes.

B Idaho enjoys an absolute advantage in growing potatoes.

C Idaho is the only state that grows potatoes.

D Idaho potatoes taste better than other varieties.

5 **To produce so many potatoes, farmers in Idaho must be extremely**

A efficient.

B thrifty.

C resourceful.

D opportunistic.

Comparative Advantage

Individuals and businesses that have a comparative advantage specialize in goods or services that are produced at a relatively low opportunity cost; that is, they produce the product or service more efficiently than other companies can.

Directions: Answer the following questions.

6 **Company A and Company B make mops and brooms. If Company A can make more mops and brooms than Company B, it has**

A a higher absolute advantage compared to Company B.

B a lower absolute advantage compared to Company B.

C an absolute advantage equal to Company B.

D an opportunity to create an absolute advantage over Company B.

7 **The law of comparative advantage says that companies with the lower opportunity cost should**

A seek an absolute advantage.

B produce fewer goods or services.

C specialize in that product or service.

D produce both goods.

✔ Test-Taking Tip

When you are reading multiple-choice questions, look for superlatives, such as *always, best,* or *never.* These indicate that the correct answer must be a very precise fact that can never be disputed. Very few questions fit that criteria.

Production of Guns and Butter

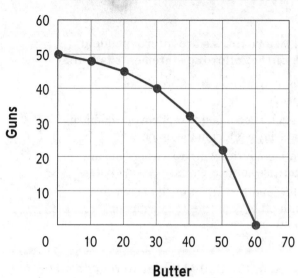

8   How many guns could be produced if no butter is produced?

A   50
B   60
C   70
D   80

9   If the same producer made guns and butter, what is the approximate number of guns that could be produced if 50 units of butter were produced?

A   0
B   about 22
C   about 35
D   about 40

10 By specializing and producing the item for which he has a comparative advantage, a gun producer could produce a maximum of

A   50 guns.
B   60 guns.
C   70 guns.
D   130 guns.

11 By specializing and producing those items for which they had a comparative advantage, separate gun and butter producers could together have a combined production possibility of

A   60 guns + 50 butter units.
B   50 guns + 60 butter units.
C   60 guns + 70 butter units.
D   70 guns + 60 butter units.

12 If 40 guns are produced, how much butter can be produced?

A   20
B   30
C   40
D   50

Interdependence

When businesses are linked to other businesses to operate, they are said to be interdependent.

Directions: Answer the following questions.

13 **When producers are interdependent, what do they share?**

A Profits

B Productivity

C Costs

D Resources

14 **What is the major risk that interdependence poses to businesses that are interdependent?**

A It is more difficult for the interdependent businesses to be profitable.

B Information is shared among the interdependent businesses.

C Productivity decreases as resources are shared.

D Disasters that hit one business harm the other business.

15 **Which of the following sets of economic factors are closely interdependent?**

A Manufacturers, shipping companies, and retailers

B Competing accounting firms

C Individuals in their roles as consumers

D Healthcare workers, laboratories, and media business

16 **When two countries are interdependent, which of the following statements is true?**

A Both countries can afford to not specialize.

B Negative economic events in one country have little effect in the other.

C Both countries will experience similar increases or decreases in productivity.

D The countries are more likely to trade with other countries than with one another.

17 **The need of the United States to rely on oil imports from the Middle East is an example of which of the following?**

A Opportunity Cost

B Interdependence

C Supply and demand

D Comparative advantage

18 **Which of the following situations is a disadvantage for a car manufacturer that is dependent on tires supplied by a firm in another country?**

A The other country starts producing its own cars.

B The car manufacturer's country puts a limit on imported cars.

C A competing car manufacturer goes out of business.

D The rubber industry workers in the other country go on strike.

This lesson will help you understand how the economic behavior of individuals and companies can be analyzed. Use it with Core Lesson 6.1 *Microeconomics* to reinforce and apply your knowledge.

Key Concept

The forces of supply and demand determine the market prices of most products and resources in the US and global economies.

Market Influences

The global market is where the forces of supply and demand exert influence over consumers.

Directions: Answer the following questions.

1 In a market economy, who has the most influence on the demand side of the market?

A Producers

B Sellers

C Buyers

D Government regulators

2 In a mixed economy,

A the forces of supply and demand have very little influence.

B the government sets prices and controls the quantities of goods and services.

C the government regulates the economy while allowing market forces to work.

D the economy is centrally planned.

3 Which of the following statements best describes how prices are set?

A Sellers set prices for goods and services.

B Buyers set prices for goods and services.

C Manufacturers set prices for goods; workers set prices for services.

D Sellers set prices, but buyers influence price changes.

4 What is the most likely effect of a product rising in price?

A Producers decrease production of the product.

B Producers make a different product.

C Producers increase production of the product.

D Consumers buy more of the product.

5 What is the term used to describe the study of the exchange between buyers and sellers?

A Macroeconomics

B Market equilibrium

C Microeconomics

D Supply and demand

6 Nations with a market economy allow which force to influence the market?

A Producers

B Supply and demand

C Government regulations

D Market equilibrium

Laws of Supply and Demand

Supply (the amount of goods and services available) and demand (how much consumers desire a product) are two concepts that are related in a free-market economy.

Directions: Questions 7 through 10 are based on the graph below.

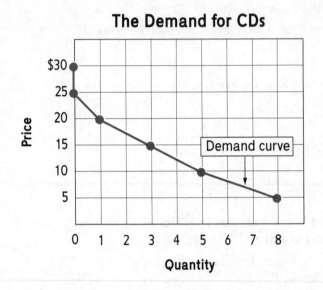

The Demand for CDs

8 How many CDs would be demanded at a price of $15.00?

    A 3

    B 5

    C 8

    D 10

9 Between which two prices did market demand increase the most?

    A $25.00–$20.00

    B $20.00–$15.00

    C $15.00–$10.00

    D $10.00–$5.00

7 What does a demand curve tell you about the relationship between the price of a good and the quantity of that good?

    A As the price rises, the quantity increases.

    B As quantity increases, price increases.

    C As price decreases, the quantity increases.

    D As quantity decreases, price decreases.

10 What is the price of CDs when 5 are demanded?

    A $5

    B $10

    C $15

    D $20

 Test-Taking Tip

Before answering questions related to a graph, be sure to identify what is represented on each axis. Then carefully check how the values on each axis increase or decrease.

11 Consider the graph below.

Price of 40″ LED Televisions

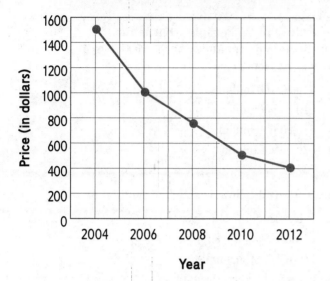

The price of televisions is decreasing over time, shown by what on the graph?

A   The supply

B   The median

C   The equilibrium

D   The trend

12 If the price of an item rises, the quantity supplied also rises. If the price drops, the quantity supplied goes down as well. Which statement explains this?

A   People do not usually buy in bulk.

B   Prices are not always a good signal.

C   The profit motive drives suppliers.

D   Sales generate more business.

13 Which statement represents a clear sign that a product's supply is greater than its demand?

A   The seller raises the product's price.

B   The seller puts the product on clearance sale.

C   The product quickly sells out in stores.

D   The consumer stands in long lines to buy the product.

14 A black market, or illegal marketplace, for products is created when there is

A   high demand for a product.

B   low demand for a product.

C   a drop in prices.

D   a reduction in regulations.

15 How does the supply of a good affect the price and quantity?

A   If the price falls, the quantity supplied also falls.

B   If the price falls, the quantity supplied rises.

C   If the price rises, the quantity supplied rises.

D   If the price rises, the quantity supplied falls.

Market Equilibrium

The aim of the market is to compromise between the interests of the buyers and the interests of the sellers, a term called *market equilibrium*, which is reached when demand is equal to the supply.

Directions: Questions 16 through 18 are based on the graph below.

Graphing the Equilibrium Price

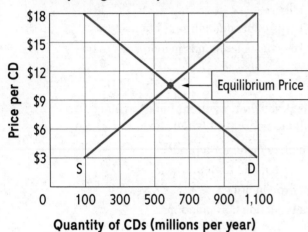

17 According to this graph, what is the equilibrium price, and how many CDs will be sold at that price?

   A $10.00/100 million

   B $10.50/600 million

   C $15.00/600 million

   D $20.00/1.1 billion

18 Market equilibrium is reached when demand

   A is less than the supply.

   B is more than the supply.

   C is equal to the supply.

   D rises faster than the supply.

16 **To illustrate market equilibrium, what information is needed on a graph?**

   A Supply—the quantity of products available

   B Supply curve—the quantity of products supplied at different prices

   C Demand curve—the quantity of products demanded at different prices

   D The supply curve and the demand curve

This lesson will help you understand how our government forms and carries out policies that affect the nation's economy. Use it with Core Lesson 6.2 *Macroeconomics and Government Policy* to reinforce and apply your knowledge.

Key Concept

The federal government uses fiscal policies and monetary policies to manage the economy.

Federal Revenue and Expenditures

The federal government collects income, mostly from taxes, to perform its operation.

Directions: Answer the following questions.

1 **Approximately half of the government's income, or revenue, comes from**

   A   income taxes.

   B   property taxes.

   C   tariffs.

   D   user fees.

2 **Government expenditures can be defined as**

   A   revenue that the government takes in.

   B   money that the government pays out.

   C   taxes, tariffs, and fees.

   D   the difference between revenue and expenses.

3 **How does the government borrow money from American citizens?**

   A   Collecting income taxes

   B   Placing tariffs on imports

   C   Selling bonds to individuals

   D   Collecting Medicare payroll deductions

4 **Consider the statement below by President Barack Obama.**

> "A key part of the rebalancing that must occur as the economy returns to full employment and beyond involves taming the federal budget deficit."

What long-term problem does this statement address?

   A   State budget shortfalls

   B   Tax increases

   C   Rising Social Security costs

   D   Growing federal debt

5 **What causes growth in the federal debt?**

   A   Payment of federal bonds

   B   Increase in federal taxes

   C   Federal borrowing

   D   Budget surpluses

Directions: Use the graph below to help answer questions 6 through 9.

Fiscal Year 2011 Budget Request

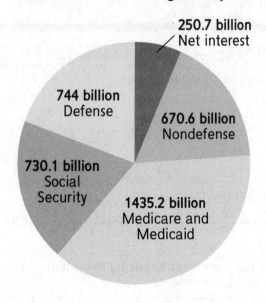

744 billion Defense

250.7 billion Net interest

670.6 billion Nondefense

730.1 billion Social Security

1435.2 billion Medicare and Medicaid

6 **According to the graph, what was most of the 2011 federal budget devoted to?**

A   Defense

B   Medicare/Medicaid

C   Net Interest

D   Social Security

7 **The smallest portion of the budget was from**

A   Defense.

B   Social Security.

C   Net interest.

D   Nondefense.

8 **Which two portions of the budget account for almost equal amounts?**

A   Defense and Social Security

B   Net interest and Nondefense

C   Defense and Medicare

D   Social Security and Net interest

9 **What do you think could cause the Net Interest to decrease?**

A   An increase in Nondefense spending

B   A decrease in the federal deficit

C   A decrease in the number of people eligible for Social Security benefits

D   A rise in Defense spending due to war

 Test-Taking Tip

Read the title of a circle graph to identify the topic. Look for labels to explain what the different slices represent.

Federal Fiscal and Monetary Policies

To manage its economy effectively, the federal government has specific plans and laws related to money supply, credit, and interest rates.

Directions: Answer the following questions.

10 **Which of the following is most likely to be taxed at the lowest rate?**

A   Alcohol

B   Cigarettes

C   Energy-efficient products

D   Gasoline

11 **What is the most likely reason that the federal government got most of its revenue from tariffs in the 1800s?**

A   The United States imported more goods in the 1800s than it does now.

B   The federal government collected a low amount of income taxes during this period.

C   Government spending was much lower at that time.

D   Local businesses did not need as much protection at that time.

12 **Why does the federal government sometimes use fiscal policy?**

A   To control the money supply

B   To withhold funds from states

C   To add to the federal debt

D   To stimulate the economy in bad times

13 **Most of the recent government subsidies have been appropriated to**

A   balance the national budget.

B   lower the cost of food products.

C   construct new bridges and roads.

D   provide aid for the unemployed.

14 **Federal regulations can have a negative effect on the economy by**

A   limiting monopolies and encouraging competition.

B   making products more expensive to manufacture.

C   discouraging efficiency and promoting waste.

D   outlawing unfair trade and pricing practices.

15 **How might a subsidy on corn affect consumers?**

A   It would increase the cost of corn to consumers.

B   It would reduce the cost of corn to consumers.

C   It would affect the quality of the corn.

D   It would decrease the supply of corn.

Directions: Questions 16 through 20 are based on the following information.

"In short, the original goal of the Great Experiment that was the founding of the Fed was the preservation of financial stability . . . How should a central bank enhance financial stability? One means is by assuming the lender-of-last-resort function . . . under which the central bank uses its power to provide liquidity to ease market conditions during periods of panic or incipient panic . . .

However, putting out the fire is not enough; it is also important to foster a financial system that is sufficiently resilient to withstand large financial shocks. Toward that end, the Federal Reserve, together with other regulatory agencies . . . is actively engaged in monitoring financial developments and working to strengthen financial institutions and markets . . . What about the monetary policy framework? In general, the Federal Reserve's policy framework . . . include[s an] emphasis on preserving the Fed's inflation credibility, which is critical for anchoring inflation expectation."

—Chairman Ben S. Bernanke at "The First 100 Years of the Federal Reserve: The Policy Record, Lessons Learned, and Prospects for the Future," a conference sponsored by the National Bureau of Economic Research, Cambridge, Massachusetts, July 10, 2013

16 **According to the passage, the primary goal of the Federal Reserve is to**

A   prevent inflation.

B   control the nation's banks.

C   preserve financial stability.

D   monitor fiscal developments.

17 **On the basis of this passage, what is meant by the Federal Reserve's "power to provide liquidity"?**

A   Its large number of reserve banks

B   Its ability to control the money supply

C   Its desire to keep the government stable

D   Its independence from the federal government

18 **During good economic times, the Federal Reserve will pursue policies designed to**

A   regulate financial institutions as little as possible.

B   reduce interest rates as low as possible.

C   control inflation as much as possible.

D   increase liquidity when available.

19 **One of the primary goals of the Federal Trade Commission is to**

A   stop unfair business practices.

B   manage the country's money supply.

C   set interest rates.

D   test all foods and medicines.

20 **Which of the following can cause market failures?**

A   Antitrust Acts

B   Bank closings because of panics

C   Imperfect competition

D   Wrong Fed decisions

This lesson will help you understand how a variety of practices help measure the health of an economy. Use it with Core Lesson 6.3 *Macroeconomics, the GDP, and Price Fluctuation* to reinforce and apply your knowledge.

Key Concept

Measures such as an economy's GDP, inflation or deflation rate, and unemployment rate provide economists with ways to measure an economy's health.

Gross Domestic Product

Gross domestic product, the value of all goods and services produced in the nation in a year, is one of the most vital measurements of a nation's economy.

Directions: Answer the following questions.

1 **A country's gross domestic product (GDP) is determined by**

A adding the quantity of goods and services to intermediate goods and services.

B multiplying the quantity of goods and services by their prices.

C adding domestic goods and services to imported goods and services.

D subtracting quantity of goods and services from government spending.

2 **What is the most likely reason that a country has a high GDP?**

A Its government spends a lot of money.

B It creates a high quantity of goods and services.

C It is a large nation with many people.

D Its products have high prices.

3 **A nation's GDP includes**

A final goods manufactured domestically.

B the sale of used goods.

C all components of final goods manufactured domestically.

D final goods manufactured domestically or abroad.

4 **In which of these countries would GDP be the least useful measure of the strength of the economy?**

A An island nation, where bartering is common

B A tiny nation that is part of the European Union

C A large Asian nation with a strong government

D A nation that participates in United States trade agreements

Directions: Use the table below to help answer questions 5 and 6.

GDP of Selected Countries, 2012

Country	GDP in 2012 (in trillion $)
Canada	1.8
China	8.4
Mexico	1.2
United Kingdom	2.4
United States	15.7

5 Which of the following is true according to the data given in this chart?

  A A barter economy is used in a certain region of Mexico.

  B China exports more goods than it imports.

  C The value of Canadian currency has increased over the last few years.

  D GDP of the United States is almost twice as much as the next closest country's GDP.

6 Which country has a GDP that is approximately twice the GDP of Mexico?

  A Canada

  B China

  C United Kingdom

  D United States

Directions: Answer the following questions.

7 Which aspect of GDP is misleading as a measure of a nation's overall well-being?

  A GDP includes negative events such as wars and natural disasters.

  B GDP includes economic activity outside organized markets.

  C GDP includes the value of goods and services from foreign countries.

  D GDP includes the value of intermediate goods, which results in unreliable figures.

8 Which of the following products would count toward United States GDP?

  A Natural gas from Canada used in Illinois

  B Seats made in Poland, to be installed in a new car in Detroit

  C California surfboards sold in Mexico

  D New American-made tires for an American-made motorcycle

 **Test-Taking Tip**

Don't get stuck on a difficult question. Instead, make a small mark next to the question. Go back and answer that question later. Other parts of the test may give you a clue that will help you answer that question.

Inflation and Deflation

Inflation and deflation can affect the GDP. As prices rise, the power of the dollar declines. As prices fall, the purchasing power of the dollar increases.

Directions: Answer the following questions.

9 The term used to describe a rise in the general level of prices over time is

   A deflation.

   B inflation.

   C integration.

   D stagflation.

10 Deflation has what effect on the value of the dollar?

   A It causes the dollar to increase in value in the short term only.

   B It causes the value of the dollar to decrease.

   C It causes the value of the dollar to increase.

   D It has no effect on the value of the dollar.

Directions: Use the graph to help answer questions 11 through 14.

Price of a Market Basket of Goods 1913 to 2013

11 If a person paid $10.00 for a market basket of goods in 1913, how much would the same goods have cost in 1983?

   A $30.00

   B $53.00

   C $98.00

   D $230.00

12 The Federal Reserve believes that 2 percent inflation is desirable. At that rate, approximately how much would this market basket of goods most likely cost in 2023?

   A $234.00

   B $245.00

   C $268.00

   D $280.00

13 During which period did inflation increase the fastest?

   A 1913 to 1923

   B 1933 to 1943

   C 1973 to 1983

   D 1993 to 2003

14 The graph is a visual representation of inflation and deflation in the American economy. During which of these years was there a period of deflation in the United States?

   A 1923

   B 1933

   C 1943

   D 1953

Unemployment

Unemployment happens when people leave their former jobs for any number of reasons and have not yet found new jobs.

Directions: Use the graph to help answer questions 15 and 16.

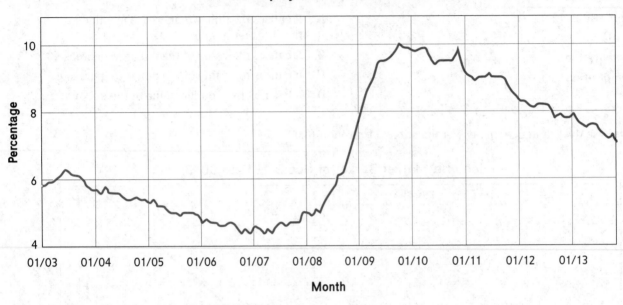

US Unemployment Rate, 2003–2013

Source: http://data.bls.gov/timeseries/LNS14000000

15 During which year represented in the graph was the United States unemployment rate highest?

   A 2008

   B 2009

   C 2010

   D 2012

16 What was the trend in the United States unemployment rate between 2007 and 2009?

   A The unemployment rate was rising.

   B The unemployment rate was steady.

   C The unemployment rate was falling.

   D The chart does not give enough information to answer.

Directions: Answer the following questions.

17 The unemployment rate is the percentage of individuals in the civilian labor force who

   A have lost their job during the current year.

   B have ceased looking for a job.

   C are actively looking for a job but cannot find one.

   D were looking for a job within the past year.

18 Businesses lay off workers during recession and hire them back in good times, causing what type of unemployment?

   A Cyclical

   B Seasonal

   C Structural

   D Technological

This lesson will help you understand major economic events in US history. Use it with Core Lesson 7.1 *Major Economic Events* to reinforce and apply your knowledge.

Key Concept

The federal government has responded to economic events in a variety of ways, for example, by developing stimulus programs and regulating businesses.

Booms and Busts

Throughout its history, the United States has experienced economic booms and busts.

Directions: Answer the following questions.

1 How can inflation weaken an economy?

    A It causes people to buy luxuries they cannot afford.

    B It leads companies to increase production, shrinking demand.

    C It reduces demand for goods, shrinking GDP.

    D It causes stocks bought on margin to drop in value.

2 Mass production had what effect on the economy in the 1920s?

    A It caused the unemployment rate to increase.

    B It lowered the prices of goods significantly.

    C It allowed an increase in middle class families.

    D It caused a trough to develop in the economy.

3 At a certain point, an increased demand for Model Ts would lead to a drop in supply. At that point, which of these is likely to have happened?

    A An increase in price

    B A decrease in inflation

    C A decline in GDP

    D An economic trough

4 Which of the following best describes the US economy from 1920 to 1929?

    A People bought less goods.

    B Wages were cut.

    C The GDP increased.

    D Federal spending increased.

5 The stock market crash of October 1929 was made worse by which of the following factors?

    A People still owed money for the stocks they owned.

    B Production in US factories had hit its peak.

    C Too many people had bought automobiles on credit.

    D The federal government had placed strict regulations on stock trading.

The Great Depression

The Great Depression was a period of severe decline in the US economy during the 1930s.

Directions: Questions 6 through 8 are based on the following information.

During the period between 1929 and 1933, more than 100,000 businesses failed, causing massive job loss. Without employment, many families lost their homes. Because almost 25 percent of American workers were out of work and homeless, shantytowns began to appear in parks and at the edges of cities. These collections of shacks were called "Hoovervilles." Although Hoovervilles were made of temporary and makeshift structures, some were organized, with a mayor and governing committees. Even after the Great Depression, Hoovervilles persisted in some areas.

6   **What is the most likely reason why Hoovervilles would have persisted beyond the Great Depression?**

   A   Strong communities were formed in these shantytowns.

   B   Some Hooverville governments were highly effective.

   C   Some people preferred living outside to living inside.

   D   Relief programs took time to help all those in need.

7   **What is the most likely reason that shantytowns were located in parks and at the edges of cities?**

   A   Building materials were more abundant there.

   B   Foreclosed homes were usually near these areas.

   C   Cities set aside these areas for the homeless.

   D   These areas were a source of public or unused land.

8   **Why were the shantytowns named Hoovervilles?**

   A   President Hoover had enacted many government programs that provided economic relief to individuals.

   B   President Hoover had been involved in the stock market crash, which had damaged the US economy.

   C   Many companies owned by Herbert Hoover had failed, increasing unemployment during the Great Depression.

   D   Massive unemployment and foreclosures occurred during Herbert Hoover's tenure as president.

The Government Responds

The federal government implemented laws and set up agencies to combat economic hardship and pull the US out of the Great Depression.

Directions: Answer the following questions.

9 Which definition fits the meaning of the term "stimulus"?

   A A period of time when the country's GDP grows

   B Government policies to provide relief to workers and businesses

   C A dramatic increase in the price of goods and services

   D A system in which the means of production are controlled by the government

10 Why did President Herbert Hoover not take steps to address the Great Depression in its early years?

   A He tried to work out a joint response with state governments.

   B He was worried that if he acted too aggressively it would hurt his chances for reelection.

   C He feared that too much government involvement amounted to socialism.

   D He was too involved in addressing foreign crises.

11 Why did farmers choose to destroy their crops in the early 1930s?

   A They thought the shortage would lead to higher demand and prices would go up.

   B They thought they could create a surplus and people would buy more food.

   C They thought the increase in supply would lower demand and people would pay more.

   D They thought this would lower costs, encouraging people to buy more.

12 The Social Security Act provided for which of the following?

   A Jobs

   B The right to join a union

   C A minimum wage

   D A pension

Directions: Questions 13 through 15 are based on the following information.

(1) Our greatest primary task is to put people to work. (2) This is no unsolvable problem if we face it wisely and courageously. (3) It can be accomplished in part by direct recruiting by the Government itself, treating the task as we would treat the emergency of a war, but at the same time, through this employment, accomplishing greatly needed projects to stimulate and reorganize the use of our natural resources . . .
(4) The task can be helped by definite efforts to raise the values of agricultural products and with this the power to purchase the output of our cities. (5) It can be helped by preventing realistically the tragedy of the growing loss through foreclosure of our small homes and our farms. (6) It can be helped by insistence that the Federal, State, and local governments act forthwith on the demand that their cost be drastically reduced. (7) It can be helped by the unifying of relief activities which today are often scattered, uneconomical, and unequal. (8) It can be helped by national planning for and supervision of all forms of transportation and of communications and other utilities which have a definitely public character. (9) There are many ways in which it can be helped, but it can never be helped merely by talking about it. (10) We must act and act quickly.

—President Franklin D. Roosevelt, First Inaugural Address, 1933

13 **Why do you think President Roosevelt felt his primary task was to put people back to work?**

  A Unemployment had created an unstable political environment.

  B He understood that the country would benefit from development projects.

  C Salaries would be saved in banks, stabilizing the financial industry.

  D Salaries provide money for food and shelter and help restart the economy.

14 **In which sentence does President Roosevelt speak of an issue that would be partially addressed by the creation of Social Security?**

  A Sentence 4

  B Sentence 5

  C Sentence 7

  D Sentence 8

15 **Which statement summarizes President Roosevelt's point of view, as outlined in his speech?**

  A The government must control all aspects of the American economy.

  B The economy can be improved through government intervention.

  C Direct monetary relief is the only way to help the poorest Americans.

  D Local and state governments are corrupt and must be reined in.

 Test-Taking Tip

When you are answering questions about a primary source passage, look for key words and facts within the question that you can then find within the passage.

This lesson will help you explain the relationship between political and economic freedoms, identify the economic causes and impacts of wars, and discuss how exploration and colonization were driven by economic factors. Use it with Core Lesson 7.2 *The Relationship Between Politics and Economics* to reinforce and apply your knowledge.

Key Concept

Politics and economics interact with each other in complex ways that affect the entire society.

Political and Economic Freedom

In the United States, the balance between personal freedom, as outlined in the Constitution, and economic freedom is frequently addressed.

Directions: Questions 1 through 3 are based on the passage below.

The time is arriving when we can have further tax reduction, when, unless we wish to hamper the people in their right to earn a living, we must have tax reform. The method of raising revenue ought not to impede the transaction of business; it ought to encourage it. I am opposed to extremely high rates, because they produce little or no revenue, because they are bad for the country, and, finally, because they are wrong. We cannot finance the country, we cannot improve social conditions, through any system of injustice, even if we attempt to inflict it upon the rich. Those who suffer the most harm will be the poor. This country believes in prosperity. It is absurd to suppose that it is envious of those who are already prosperous. The wise and correct course to follow in taxation and all other economic legislation is not to destroy those who have already secured success but to create conditions under which everyone will have a better chance to be successful.

—President Calvin Coolidge, Inaugural Address, 1925

1 **President Coolidge suggests that higher taxes will affect the poor the most because they will**

A not have access to government programs.

B have the highest tax burden of all citizens.

C be limited in their economic opportunities.

D become envious of the rich, giving rise to class warfare.

3 **Which of these statements does the speech appear to support?**

A The poor will benefit most from larger taxes on the rich.

B Prosperity cannot be attained unless taxation is increased.

C Successful people should not be punished through taxation.

D The tax system should be completely abolished in the United States.

2 **Which of these is an inference about President Coolidge's beliefs that can be made from this speech?**

A Poor people are jealous of rich people.

B Rich people earned their success.

C Taxation is completely unnecessary.

D Poor people have been treated justly.

Directions: Answer the following questions.

4 President Franklin Roosevelt's economic policy differed from President Coolidge's approach in that Roosevelt

A promoted limited government intervention in economic affairs.

B set the ground rules for free enterprise and then left the market alone.

C created government programs to put people to work and to stimulate the economy.

D favored a redistribution of wealth in which personal fortunes would be limited.

5 In the late 1800s, the United States began looking for new markets for goods produced. Why did the government look for new markets?

A The United States wanted to become a major world power.

B The United States produced more goods than Americans could buy.

C The United States wanted to gain political influence over other nations.

D The United States needed to form defensive alliances in other parts of the world.

6 When war occurs in a country, which of these is a common economic effect for its citizens?

A a decline in poverty

B an increase in resources

C a decrease in jobs

D a surplus of goods

7 What is most likely to happen to a country's economy if the value of its currency goes down?

A Its exports go up because they become cheaper.

B Its imports go down because they become cheaper.

C It gains export jobs because labor becomes less costly.

D Workers benefit because prices go down.

8 Which of these is a problem with market economics?

A They are inefficient.

B They cycle through periods of growth and decline.

C They often result in shortages of consumer goods.

D They tend to have lower GDP per capita.

The Politics of Imperialism

The policy of imperialism—the governing of weaker nations or colonies by more powerful nations—is an example of the influence of politics on the economy.

Directions: Answer the following questions.

9 **Which of the following is an example of an open-door policy?**

   A Hawaii was added to the United States as a territory in 1898.

   B The United States obtains territory to build a canal in Panama.

   C The United States and Mexico have the right to trade with China.

   D Sugar from Brazil is taxed when it enters the United States.

10 **Which of the following definitions fits the meaning of the term "annexation"?**

   A A territory is transferred from one power to another by treaty.

   B One country takes control of another country or territory.

   C One country offers military support to a weaker neighbor.

   D A mutually beneficial trading relationship exists between two countries.

Directions: Questions 11 and 12 are based on the passage below.

I, Liliuokalani of Hawaii, by the will of God named heir apparent on the tenth day of April, A.D. 1877, and by the grace of God Queen of the Hawaiian Islands on the seventeenth day of January, A.D. 1893, do hereby protest against the ratification of a certain treaty, which, so I am informed, has been signed at Washington by Messrs. Hatch, Thurston, and Kinney, purporting to cede those Islands to the territory and dominion of the United States. I declare such a treaty to be an act of wrong toward the native and part-native people of Hawaii, an invasion of the rights of the ruling chiefs, in violation of international rights both toward my people and toward friendly nations with whom they have made treaties, the perpetuation of the fraud whereby the constitutional government was overthrown, and, finally, an act of gross injustice to me.

—Queen Liliuokalani of Hawaii, Official Protest to the Treaty of Annexation, 1897

11 **What does Queen Liliuokalani imply about her role as ruler of Hawaii?**

   A She was ordained by God to rule.

   B She was chosen by the people to rule.

   C She supports American rule of Hawaii.

   D She needs help from the US government.

12 **Why does Queen Liliuokalani protest the treaty referred to in the passage?**

   A It gives native Hawaiians more say in their government.

   B It ignores the right of Hawaii to rule itself independently.

   C It spreads imperialism into the South Pacific region.

   D It overthrows the constitutional government of Hawaii.

✔ Test-Taking Tip

An inference is a conclusion that is reached on the basis of evidence and reasoning. When you are asked to identify an inference based on evidence from a reading passage, first read the inferences that are provided. Then read the passage to see which inference could be made based on information in the passage.

The Economics of War

War and economics are interconnected. Economic disputes have been the cause of many wars throughout history. In addition, all wars have a significant economic impact on the people and nations involved in those wars.

Directions: Answer the following questions.

13 Which of these impacts of war could indirectly cause homelessness?

  A Bombing destroys houses.

  B War disrupts businesses.

  C Fighting destroys farm fields.

  D Conflict shuts down power grids.

14 A newly installed government in a country torn by war would be advised to

  A encourage banks to begin lending.

  B encourage companies to start hiring.

  C seek foreign aid to stabilize the government.

  D seek military aid to secure the government.

Directions: Questions 15 and 16 are based on the passage below.

The United States has a long history of extending a helping hand to people overseas struggling to make a better life. It is a history that both reflects the American people's compassion and support of human dignity as well as advances US foreign policy interests.

—US Agency for International Development, Statement of "Who We Are"

15 To improve the lives of people in foreign countries that may have been affected by war or famine, the United States often provides

  A foreign donors.

  B humanitarian aid.

  C military aid.

  D policy initiatives.

16 How would US aid advance its foreign policy interests?

  A By providing military support to foreign countries

  B By supporting those who want to overthrow dictators

  C By stabilizing economies of foreign countries

  D By showing that US citizens can be compassionate

This lesson will help you understand how the Scientific and Industrial Revolutions have shaped modern life. Use it with Core Lesson 7.3 *The Scientific and Industrial Revolutions* to reinforce and apply your knowledge.

Key Concept

Today's world has been shaped by the technological advances that came about as a result of the Scientific and Industrial Revolutions.

The Scientific Revolution

During the Scientific Revolution, which lasted from the late 1500s to the early 1600s, people began to use rational thinking to question old ideas about the world around them and to search for new answers.

Directions: Answer the following questions.

1 **The series of experiments and observations scientists use to arrive at their conclusions is called**

   A innovation.

   B the scientific method.

   C technology.

   D process of elimination.

2 **The Scientific Revolution is referred to as a "revolution" because it**

   A lasted for close to a century.

   B caused the overthrow of many governments.

   C led to violent conflicts between countries.

   D caused sudden and dramatic change.

3 **The tool of navigation that showed the direction of magnetic north was the**

   A caravel.

   B compass.

   C carrack.

   D quadrant.

4 **Which of the following scientists made discoveries related to the human body?**

   A Galileo Galilei

   B Isaac Newton

   C Nicholas Copernicus

   D Antonie van Leeuwenhoek

5 **What are the roles of facts and theories in the scientific method?**

   A Scientists test facts by applying theories.

   B Scientists use the scientific method to organize facts and test theories.

   C In the scientific method, facts are general statements used to explain observable theories.

   D Scientists create theories by resolving conflicting facts.

Directions: Questions 6 and 7 are based on the following information.

The astrolabe is an instrument that allows the user to study the position of the Sun and stars in order to determine time during the day or night and the time of a celestial event. During the 15th and 16th centuries, the Mariner's Astrolabe was developed to measure the height of a celestial body above the horizon.

6 An astrolabe would allow a navigator to determine which of these while sailing in the middle of an ocean?

A Distance to land

B Time until sunrise

C Latitude position

D Distance between stars

7 The invention of the astrolabe had the greatest effect on which of the following?

A The Scientific Revolution

B Industrialization

C European exploration

D The work of Copernicus and Galileo

The Industrial Revolution

During the time period known as the Industrial Revolution, machines replaced hand tools in the manufacturing of goods, and many people left their farms to work in factories.

Directions: Answer the following questions.

8 What is the most likely effect of an industrial revolution in a country?

A People move from the cities to rural areas.

B The economy shifts from agriculture to manufacturing.

C New machines make more expensive goods that are difficult to obtain.

D More people are able to work at home.

9 Why did inventions such as the flying shuttle and the spinning machine lead to the end of the cottage industry system?

A People were not needed to run these machines.

B The machines were too large and complex to be operated in private homes.

C Government regulations prohibited families from owning these machines.

D The machines were dangerous for children to operate.

10 How did India contribute to Britain's success in becoming an industrial society?

A It provided iron to make machines.

B It provided coal to run steam engines.

C It provided raw cotton for the textile mills.

D It provided people to work in manufacturing.

11 Which factor of production was most significant in allowing Britain to run the newly invented steam engines?

A Coal

B Iron

C Raw materials

D Workers

Cotton Mills in England, 1838

Location in England	Number of Cotton Mills	Number of Employees
Northwest	1,562	215,556
Northeast	16	1,704
Southwest	1	29
Southeast	19	942

12 The movement of people from farms to industrial cities appears to have been greatest in which region of England?

A   Northwest

B   Northeast

C   Southwest

D   Southeast

13 Based on the information in the table, you can conclude that in the first half of the 19th century, northwest England most likely developed a higher concentration of

A   universities.

B   middle-class families.

C   labor unions.

D   railroads.

14 Great Britain's colonies helped it change from an agricultural to an industrial society by providing

A   the coal that fueled the machines in British factories.

B   inventions that created new ways of producing goods.

C   the labor force needed for British factories.

D   raw materials that were processed into finished products.

15 Which of the following inventions do you think were most important to the growth of cities in the interior of the United States?

A   The telegraph

B   The cotton gin

C   The locomotive

D   Slave codes

✓ Test-Taking Tip

When you are answering questions based on a data table, study the table to determine any trends in the data.

The Rise of Cities

Between 1800 and 1850 there was a significant increase in the number and size of cities in Europe and the United States.

Directions: Answer the following questions.

16 One factor that caused farmworkers to move to larger cities during the Industrial Revolution was

    A unhealthy living conditions.

    B increases in technology.

    C labor unions.

    D settlement houses.

17 Which of the following situations led to the rapid growth of cities in the early 1800s?

    A Workers needed to live close to their jobs in the factories and mills.

    B The suburbs were overcrowded, so people had to move into urban areas.

    C Trains made it easier for workers from the cities to get to their jobs on the farms.

    D The growth of the cottage industry system led to the construction of new houses.

18 Before labor unions formed during the Industrial Revolution, which of these statements was true?

    A Employers were held responsible for workplace accidents.

    B Employee wages were based on experience and gender.

    C Employers operated according to their company's set of rules.

    D Employees working long hours received overtime pay.

Directions: Questions 19 and 20 are based on the following information.

Textile factories in England used child labor to perform many tasks, such as picking up loose cotton or crawling under machines while they were in motion. Interviews with people who worked in cotton mills as children reveal that they were sometimes forced to work from 12 to 17 hours at the mill and were punished if they tried to sit down or rest in any way. Very small children were sought for mill work, because they were cheaper to hire as well as small and agile.

19 Which of these jobs in a cotton mill would most likely be done by the youngest or smallest children?

    A Picking up cotton from the floor

    B Cleaning cloth-making machinery

    C Running errands for managers

    D Crawling under running machines

20 According to the passage, which statement best describes conditions during the Industrial Revolution?

    A Poverty was common.

    B Education was valued.

    C Illness was common.

    D Children were valued.

This lesson will help you learn what banks do and how you can use them. Use it with Core Lesson 8.1 *Savings and Banking* to reinforce and apply your knowledge.

Key Concept

Financial institutions provide consumers with services such as checking and savings accounts to help them manage their money.

Banks

Banks are in business to make a profit. They do that by providing three basic services—keeping money safe, transferring funds, and loaning money.

Directions: Answer the following questions.

1 Which of these is an unsafe method of transferring money and a practice that banks will never use?

A Automatic withdrawals for bill payment

B Sending cash through insured mail

C Electronic funds transfer

D Checking accounts

2 What three basic services do banks provide?

A Keeping money safe, charging fees for services, and loaning money

B Keeping money safe, transferring funds, and charging fees for services

C Charging fees for services, transferring funds, and loaning money

D Keeping money safe, transferring funds, and loaning money

3 Banks lend out most of their depositors' money; the rest of the deposits are called

A reserves.

B loans.

C accounts.

D cash.

4 Writing a personal check is an example of using a bank's ability to

A safeguard money.

B make deposits.

C transfer money.

D loan money.

Directions: Questions 5 and 6 are based on the statement below.

The National Equity Bank has announced that it has more than $450 billion in cash reserves.

5 **By making this announcement regarding its cash reserves, the National Equity Bank is advertising its ability to**

   A cover depositors' withdrawals.

   B purchase competing banks.

   C pay interest on debts.

   D offer loans.

6 **The cash reserves of this bank will be**

   A used to pay its employees.

   B used to market new products and services.

   C loaned to other individuals and businesses.

   D set aside for future use.

Types of Banks

Over time, several types of banking institutions arose to serve specific needs. Today most financial institutions serve all of those needs.

Directions: Answer the following questions.

7 **What was the original purpose of a credit union?**

   A To help individuals buy homes

   B To serve the needs of businesses

   C To provide commercial accounts

   D To serve its members with emergency loans

8 **What trend has affected the initial purpose of different financial institutions?**

   A Most financial institutions today offer the same services.

   B Credit unions require members to live in the same community.

   C Savings and loans provide the most money for new home buyers.

   D Commercial banks outnumber all other financial institutions combined.

9 **Consumers generally trust that their banks will not lose their money because**

   A banks have unlimited resources.

   B banks buy insurance to cover losses.

   C consumers know their local bankers.

   D consumers are uninformed about their deposits.

10 **How do banks earn a profit?**

   A They charge customers more to borrow money than they pay to customers who save.

   B They only loan money to individuals and businesses with excellent credit ratings.

   C They transfer funds to overseas banks that pay greater interest.

   D They invest customers' savings in the stock market.

Savings banks
Credit unions
Cooperative banks

11 **What was the original purpose of the institutions shown here?**

  A To issue credit cards

  B To meet the needs of businesses

  C To offer emergency loans

  D To meet the needs of ordinary people

12 **Customers of these three institutions were originally people who**

  A safeguard money.

  B had low incomes.

  C were not served by commercial banks.

  D needed a loan.

Personal Banking

Your bank offers to protect your money, and it also offers many services, some of which might require paying a fee.

Directions: Answer the following questions.

13 **If you have a personal checking account, you can**

  A pay bills late.

  B earn a large amount of interest.

  C have someone write a check using your name.

  D withdraw money by writing a check or using an ATM.

14 **Why is it important to keep track of the account balance in your checking account?**

  A To let the bank know how much money is in your account

  B To avoid having your account temporarily closed by the bank

  C To avoid a penalty fee for writing a check for more than the balance

  D To make certain the bank has enough insurance to cover the balance of your account

15 **Every reputable bank is required to**

  A publicize consumer account information.

  B protect consumer privacy.

  C offer savings incentives.

  D offer free checking.

16 **When you write a check for more than the balance in your checking account, the bank will probably**

  A forgive you, if it is the first time.

  B close your account temporarily.

  C charge you a penalty fee.

  D hold the check until you have enough money in the account.

Directions: Questions 17 through 20 are based on the graphic below.

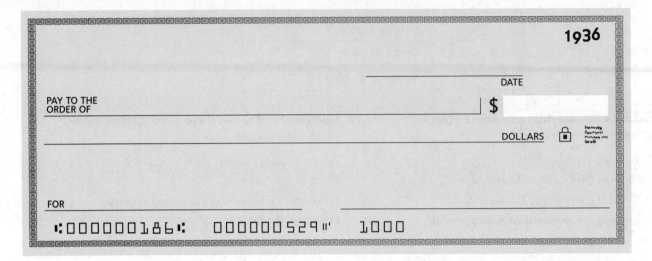

17 On December 12, 2014, Clara Partridge needs to write a check to the Leadville Water Co. in the amount of $153.23. What should she write on the line that begins "Pay to the Order Of"?

   A   Clara Partridge

   B   December 12, 2014

   C   Leadville Water Company

   D   One hundred fifty-three and 23/100

18 What information must be added to the back of this check for it to be cashed?

   A   The recipient's account number

   B   The account holder's signature

   C   The account holder's address

   D   The recipient's signature

19 What does "payable on demand" mean in regard to checking accounts?

   A   The bank must immediately transfer funds electronically.

   B   The bank must pay the amount of a check in currency.

   C   The bank must pay the amount of a check immediately.

   D   The bank must not charge interest.

20 Which number on this check designates the specific bank for this checking account?

   A   1936

   B   000000186

   C   000000529

   D   1000

 Test-Taking Tip

If more than once choice for a multiple-choice question seems correct, ask yourself if each choice completely answers the question. If a choice is only partially true, it is probably not the correct answer.

This lesson will help you identify several basic types of consumer credit, compare the different types of consumer credit, and describe situations in which each type of credit is useful. Use it with Core Lesson 8.2 *Types of Consumer Credit* to reinforce and apply your knowledge.

Key Concept

Different types of credit have different purposes and different advantages and disadvantages.

Credit

Credit allows you to own something you want or need and pay for it later. It is a convenient way to purchase, but a threat to lower your ability to purchase what you might need in the future.

Directions: Answer the following questions.

1 **If you buy a car on a secured loan and fail to make a number of payments,**

  A your credit score will increase.

  B your car will be seized.

  C the payments will be deducted from your bank.

  D the value of your car will decrease.

2 **How do credit card companies such as banks earn most of their money?**

  A By charging consumers interest and fees on their debts

  B By adding a few percentage points to the cost of items sold

  C By charging participating retail outlets 5 percent on each sale

  D By selling their credit cards to consumers

3 **Why might it be important to obtain your credit report periodically?**

  A It sometimes allows you to delay payment of bills.

  B It prevents creditors from seizing property.

  C It allows you to determine whether someone is using your identity.

  D It provides valuable information to banks and credit card companies.

4 **A home equity loan is a secured loan that might help reduce your taxes if**

  A your credit score is high.

  B the interest is tax deductible.

  C it is used for a large purchase.

  D you pay a lot in interest.

Directions: Study the chart. Then answer questions 5 through 8.

The following chart shows Mr. Fernandez's credit score from 2009 to 2012.

Year	Credit Score
2009	560
2010	620
2011	500
2012	540

5 Which of the following definitions fits the meaning of the term "credit score"?

   A A bonus from banks when you pay your bills on time

   B A report by a credit agency of how consistently you pay your bills

   C A kind of credit card that allows you to defer payment for a year

   D A way of buying something before paying for it

6 Between 2010 and 2011, Mr. Fernandez most likely

   A earned more money.

   B obtained a low-interest credit card.

   C purchased a new home.

   D missed credit card payments.

7 In 2012, Mr. Fernandez probably found that

   A he had a more difficult time getting credit.

   B interest rates were lower than they had been.

   C the cost of living was increasing rapidly.

   D he no longer had a secure source of income.

8 The credit agency that issued Mr. Fernandez's credit scores most likely obtained its information from

   A employers and retail stores.

   B the Internal Revenue Service and employers.

   C financial institutions and Social Security records.

   D banks and credit card companies.

Directions: Answer the following questions.

9 Extensive home repairs are usually best financed with home equity loans because

   A if you default, your home cannot be taken.

   B they are the best way to build your credit score.

   C interest rates are lower and often tax deductible.

   D the payment schedules are flexible.

10 You are legally allowed to obtain a free credit report

   A once per year.

   B when applying for credit.

   C when any item has been added to that report.

   D when your credit has been used illegally by another person.

Comparing Types of Credit

Different types of credit have different advantages and disadvantages.

Directions: Answer the following questions.

11 You should probably not buy a car on a credit card because credit card companies

    A do not lend large amounts of money.

    B expect repayment within a short time.

    C usually charge high interest rates.

    D will report defaults to credit agencies.

12 An installment loan to buy a home is a good idea, if a person has a down payment and

    A interest rates are high.

    B the property value is declining.

    C the home is a large one.

    D the buyer has a reliable source of income.

13 The amount you pay to use credit is the

    A annual percentage rate.

    B finance charge.

    C balance.

    D interest rate.

14 Large purchases such as homes or cars are usually obtained using

    A unsecured loans.

    B credit cards.

    C secured loans.

    D revolving credit.

15 You can avoid paying any interest on a credit card account by

    A maintaining a high credit score.

    B paying off the card's balance every month.

    C obtaining a no-interest credit card.

    D keeping a balance of under $100 at all times.

16 Under the Truth in Lending Act, creditors must disclose a loan's

    A finance charge and the annual percentage rate.

    B annual percentage rate and incentives.

    C annual percentage rate and rate of return.

    D finance charge and incentives.

17 The annual percentage rate offered by a lender

    A must match those offered by other lenders.

    B is directly established by the Federal Reserve.

    C must remain the same for the life of a loan.

    D can vary and should be compared to those offered by other lenders.

Directions: Questions 18 through 21 are based on the following information.

A recent study done by two professors at The Ohio State University indicates that younger people are more at risk from credit card debt. For example, a person born between 1980 and 1984 has debt higher than the previous two generations—$5,689 higher than their parents, and $8,156 higher than their grandparents.

"Our projections are that the typical credit card holder among younger Americans who keeps a balance will die still in debt to credit card companies."

18 Total credit card debt in the United States is a detriment to our economic future. This is a serious concern because research shows that

   A the problem seems to be getting more severe with each generation.

   B few people are paying down their credit card debt before they die.

   C credit card interest continues to rise.

   D credit card companies will be less likely to lend to younger people.

19 What can you infer from the passage about the willingness of credit card companies to offer credit to younger people?

   A Credit card companies are waiting until potential customers are older to offer their products and services to those customers.

   B Credit card companies want their younger customers to pay off credit card balances each month.

   C Credit card companies are becoming more strict about the need for potential new customers to have high credit scores.

   D Credit card companies see younger people as a good market for more of their products and services.

20 The fact that young people are buying more on credit than their parents and grandparents did most likely indicates that

   A the cost of living is lower than it used to be.

   B cash is not as available as it used to be.

   C the cost of both "wants" and "needs" has increased.

   D wages are higher than they were in the past.

21 After noting the differences between the debt of people compared to that of their parents and grandparents, how much higher would the next generation's debt be than that of their great-grandparents, assuming the trend remains the same?

   A $5,689

   B $8,156

   C $10,623

   D $11,378

 Test-Taking Tip

When you read a passage during a test, you need to eliminate information that is not necessary for answering questions. One way to do this is to read the passage, taking notes of important information, and then reviewing the questions to see what information is covered and what is not.

This lesson will help you understand the importance of consumer credit laws such as the Equal Credit Opportunity Act, the Consumer Credit Protection Act, and the Truth in Lending Act. Use it with Core Lesson 8.3 *Consumer Credit Laws* to reinforce and apply your knowledge.

Key Concept

The federal government enforces laws that provide many safeguards for the consumer using credit.

Consumer Credit Protections

Since the 1960s, the federal government has passed a variety of consumer credit protection laws to prevent discrimination, ensure that consumers have clear information about the terms of credit, and limit fees and interest rates that lenders can charge.

Directions: Questions 1 and 2 are based on the information below.

If . . . the consumer requests a copy of a consumer report from the person who procured the report, then, within 3 business days of receiving the consumer's request, together with proper identification, the person must send or provide to the consumer a copy of a report and a copy of the consumer's rights as prescribed by the Bureau . . .

A consumer may elect to have the consumer's name and address excluded from any list provided by a consumer reporting agency under subsection (c)(1)(B) in connection with a credit or insurance transaction that is not initiated by the consumer, by notifying the agency in accordance with paragraph (2).

—The Fair Credit Reporting Act

1 **The Fair Credit Reporting Act and its amendments include several provisions, such as**

A allowing consumers access to their credit reports.

B protections against exceeding a credit limit.

C protection from discrimination on the basis of race, sex, or religion.

D the right to a free credit report each month.

2 **What type of consumer safety protection was written into the Fair Credit Reporting Act that could prevent identity theft?**

A Quick prosecution of credit reporting fraud

B Addition of names from a consumer reporting agency

C Removal of the complete credit card number from receipts

D Quick responses to consumer requests for credit reports

Directions: Answer the questions below.

3 Which act limits a consumer's <u>liability</u>, or legal responsibility, for purchases if a credit card is stolen and used by someone else?

- **A** Fair Credit Billing Act
- **B** Fair Credit Reporting Act
- **C** Truth in Lending Act
- **D** Equal Credit Opportunity Act

4 Which act prohibits discrimination in credit transactions based on race, religion, sex, national origin, age, or marital or economic status?

- **A** Fair Credit Billing Act
- **B** Fair Credit Reporting Act
- **C** Truth in Lending Act
- **D** Equal Credit Opportunity Act

5 Under which act would Congress add additional consumer protection laws that relate to credit?

- **A** Fair Credit Billing Act
- **B** Consumer Credit Protection Act
- **C** Equal Credit Opportunity Act
- **D** Truth in Lending Act

Directions: Questions 6 and 7 are based on the information below.

Dear Editor:

The federal government has tried to protect credit cardholders for years. But problems persist. For example, retailers continue to approve "over the limit" purchases that often result in huge fees from the credit card companies. These companies impose a retroactive interest rate of 25 to 30 percent if a cardholder is one day late! They advertise "No Interest for 6 Months" and then charge huge interest rates if the balance isn't then paid in full. How is a person supposed to get out of debt if penalty rates are 40 percent? We need new legislation to prevent these companies from misleading the public.

Sincerely,
J.Q. Public

6 The writer believes that which of the following has not been effective?

- **A** The Fair Credit and Charge Card Disclosure Act
- **B** The Truth in Lending Act
- **C** The Credit CARD Act
- **D** Consumer Financial Protection Bureau

7 The writer believes that federal credit card protection has been

- **A** inadequate to deal with the problems facing cardholders.
- **B** too tough on credit card companies.
- **C** able to deal with all but a few cardholder problems.
- **D** unenforced since the early 1960s.

Recent Credit Protections

The federal government expanded credit protections in the 1980s and 2000s.

Directions: Answer the questions below.

8 **The Fair Credit and Charge Card Disclosure Act requires credit card providers to**

    A lower interest rates and late fees.

    B give information about their card's APR and fees.

    C issue credit cards to all applicants.

    D discard minimum monthly fees.

9 **Which question should a prospective credit card owner know the answer to?**

    A "What are the cash advance features?"

    B "What is the APR?"

    C "Are there frequent-flyer miles?"

    D "How much is the over-the-credit-limit fee?"

10 **First-time credit card users often have a different _____ than longtime users of credit cards.**

    A Payment schedule

    B APR

    C Annual fee

    D Credit limit

11 **Credit card providers are prohibited from offering which one of the following incentives?**

    A Rebates

    B No-interest loans

    C Insurance

    D Frequent-flyer miles

The Consumer Financial Protection Bureau

The government created the Consumer Financial Protection Bureau to oversee federal consumer protection laws and to look out for the interests of consumers in the financial market.

Directions: Answer the questions below.

12 **The Consumer Financial Protection Bureau (CFPB) has authority over most federal consumer protection laws and looks out for the interests of which consumers?**

    A Those with limited income

    B Those shopping for financial products or services

    C Those who have filed for bankruptcy protection

    D Those shopping for high-value products or services

13 **Before the creation of the Consumer Financial Protection Bureau, what was the main focus of government agencies in the financial marketplace?**

    A Bank safety and monetary policy

    B Protecting the interests of the credit-card industry

    C Promoting more consumer use of lending institutions

    D Maintaining low interest rates for consumer loans

Directions: Study the table below to help answer questions 14 through 17.

Credit Card Information

New balance	$3,000.00
Minimum payment due	$90.00
Payment due date	4/20/12

Late Payment Warning: If we do not receive your minimum payment by the date listed above, you may have to pay a $35 late fee and your APR may be increased up to the Penalty APR of 28.99%.

Minimum Payment Warning: If you make only the minimum payment each period, you will pay more in interest and it will take you longer to pay off your balance. For example:

If you make no additional charges using this card and each month you pay...	You will pay off the balance shown on this statement in about...	And you will end up paying an estimated total of...
Only the minimum payment	11 years	$4,745
$103	3 years	$3,712 (Savings = $1,033)

14 Why would it take 11 years to pay off the balance, if the consumer paid only the minimum payment each month on a $3,000.00 balance?

A The credit card provider can add late fees to the balance each moth.

B $3,000.00 divided by $103.00 is 132, the number of months in 11 years.

C The credit card provider would add interest to the balance each month.

D $4750.00 divided by $90.00 is 132, the number of months in 11 years.

15 To avoid any interest charges, the consumer should pay

A the balance of $3,000.00.

B the minimum payment of $90.00.

C the suggested payment of $103.00.

D the amount of $1,000.00.

16 The notices on this statement reflect a number of changes created by the Consumer Financial Protection Bureau. Which of the following caused the creation of this Bureau?

A Failure of the previous agency concerned with consumer credit laws

B Irresponsible behavior of all Americans who had made loans

C Failure of the Dodd-Frank Wall Street Reform and Consumer Protection Act

D Severe financial crisis in the United States that began in 2007

17 Based on current federal protections, you can predict that this consumer's next payment due date will most likely be on which date?

A 5/1/12

B 5/20/12

C 5/31/12

D 4/20/13

 Test-Taking Tip

When you are using a chart, first read the title of the chart to find out the topic. Then read the row and column headings to see how the chart is organized. Finally, skim the information in the chart to see whether you can make any generalizations about it.

This lesson will help you understand the development of ancient North Africa and the Indian subcontinent, early Chinese civilization, and ancient Greece and Rome. Use it with Core Lesson 9.1 *Development of Ancient Civilizations* to reinforce and apply your knowledge.

Key Concept

Ancient civilizations shared the same six developments: cities, central government, religion, social and economic classes, art and architecture, and writing.

Ancient North Africa and the Indian Subcontinent

Ancient civilizations sprang up in North Africa along the banks of the Nile River and on the Indian subcontinent along the banks of the Indus and Ganges Rivers.

Directions: Use the map below of Egyptian archaeological sites to help answer questions 1 through 4.

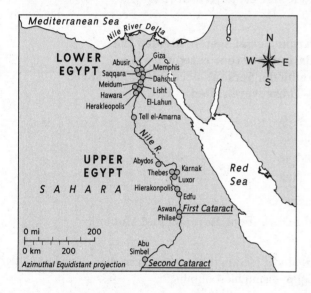

2 The placement of sites on this map shows how the development of early civilizations depended heavily on

   A stone architecture.

   B mountains.

   C access to water.

   D religious monuments.

3 Egyptians built pyramids and temples

   A near the Nile delta.

   B on the shores of the Red Sea.

   C to house government documents.

   D to defend against invasion.

1 Ancient Egypt is sometimes called the "gift of the Nile," because

   A Egypt depended on the Nile for transportation.

   B the Nile's annual floodwaters made agriculture possible.

   C the Nile is the world's longest river.

   D fishing was one of Egypt's largest industries.

4 The number of pyramids and temples among the archaeological sites shown on this map reflects the importance Egyptians placed on

   A mathematics.

   B democracy.

   C philosophy.

   D religion.

Directions: Answer the questions below.

5 Civilization developed in present-day Iraq

A after colonization by Egyptians.

B far from any body of water.

C supported by trade instead of agriculture.

D along the Tigris and Euphrates Rivers.

6 Which pharaoh was buried in the Great Pyramid of Giza?

A Tutankhamun

B Menes

C Khufu

D Narmer

7 The economies of the ancient Egyptian and Indian subcontinent civilizations were dependent upon

A trade.

B manufacturing.

C agriculture.

D hunting.

8 The Egyptian pharaoh was considered to be divine, as he represented which deity?

A Ra

B Osiris

C Anubis

D Isis

9 The Aryans significantly influenced the Indus Valley civilization by introducing

A art.

B economics.

C social structure.

D farming.

10 What did early civilizations on the Indian subcontinent have in common with ancient Egyptian civilization?

A Both built large religious monuments.

B Both began around 2500 BC.

C Both had indoor plumbing and running water.

D Both were centered near rivers.

11 The Aryan social system divided the population into four categories that determined a person's occupation and social class. These were called

A castes.

B clans.

C sudras.

D khans.

12 The inhabitants of Harappa and Mohenjo-Daro

A created a language very similar to that of Egypt, using hieroglyphics.

B spoke a language inherited from early Chinese civilizations.

C spoke separate languages influenced by different earlier civilizations.

D used a written language that has never been deciphered.

Early Chinese Civilizations

Chinese civilization was based on dynasties, and family was important to the structure of Chinese society.

Directions: Questions 13 through 15 are based on the information below.

The Mandate of Heaven

To understand almost every aspect of Chinese culture, one must understand the concept of the Mandate of Heaven. It explains the dynastic cycles in China over the centuries beginning around the 11th century B.C.

The Duke of Zhou, younger brother of King Wu of the Western Zhou dynasty, first explained the Mandate of Heaven's four principles: 1. The right to rule is granted by Heaven. 2. There is one Heaven, therefore only one ruler. 3. The right to rule depends on the virtue of the ruler. 4. The right to rule is not limited to one dynasty. In other words, a ruler may lose the Mandate of Heaven. The Zhou dynasty explained its overthrow of the Shang dynasty, based on the Mandate.

13 As is it used in this passage, the term <u>mandate</u> most likely means

A   wish.

B   command.

C   blessing.

D   favor.

14 Based on the mandate's four principles, you can assume that opponents of the Shang dynasty thought that the dynasty

A   was not virtuous.

B   descended from Heaven.

C   was an important part of Chinese culture.

D   should share its power.

15 Based on information in this passage and what you know about ancient Egypt, you can conclude that the ruling dynasties of ancient Egypt and ancient China

A   thought that life after death was similar to life on Earth.

B   believed that their authority came from a divine source.

C   presented their rulers as living gods on Earth.

D   felt that overthrowing a ruler could be justified.

Directions: Answer the questions below.

16 The ancient Chinese called the Huang He the "river of sorrows" because of what?

A   Its inability to support life due to high salinity

B   The seasonal droughts that caused the river to run dry

C   Its use as an invasion route by foreign armies

D   The regular flooding that resulted in loss of life

17 The Shang people practiced a religion that involved the worship of which of the following?

A   Ancestors

B   Objects in nature

C   A single god

D   Their king

Ancient Greece and Rome

The ancient civilizations of Greece and Rome were located in the Mediterranean region. Like other ancient civilizations, they also developed in river valleys.

Directions: Answer the questions below.

18 **How did geography contribute to the rise of the Greek polis?**

   A Rivers created transportation networks that allowed Athens to influence other areas.

   B Greece's closeness to the Near East influenced the development of the city-state.

   C Geographic barriers separated people, allowing them to develop independent city-states.

   D Greece's resources spurred trade and interaction among groups.

19 **The city-state in ancient Greece was usually built at the site of what geographic feature?**

   A A lake

   B A valley

   C A hill

   D A mountain

20 **The Greek city-state that was most important in the development of democracy was**

   A Sparta.

   B Corinth.

   C Athens.

   D Byzantium.

21 **By the third century B.C., the government of the Roman Republic, like the government of ancient Athens,**

   A allowed male citizens to participate in government.

   B forbid citizens from interfering in economic matters.

   C required male citizens to own land to participate in government.

   D gave citizens the right to veto the actions of the Senate.

22 **Romans established a republic, which is a system of government in which citizens**

   A govern directly through voting.

   B elect representatives to govern.

   C chosen by one leader make most decisions.

   D choose an emperor to govern.

23 **Which of the following best explains the difference between the governments of ancient Egypt and China with those of ancient Greece and Rome?**

   A The governments of Greece and Rome did not recognize a class system.

   B The governments of Greece and Rome were not based on agriculture.

   C The governments of Greece and Rome allowed ordinary citizens to participate.

   D The governments of Greece and Rome had no official rulers.

✓ Test-Taking Tip

If you can't identify all of the correct answers in a question, begin with the one or two that you know. Eliminate the choices that you know are incorrect, and then select the best option from the remaining choices.

This lesson will help you understand boundaries and borders, why borders often follow natural features, and how cooperation and conflict influence the division of Earth's surface. Use it with Core Lesson 9.2 *Nationhood and Statehood* to reinforce and apply your knowledge.

Key Concept

Political and geographic boundaries divide Earth into different regions and nations.

Boundaries and Borders

Boundaries are lines that separate one area of Earth from another area.

Directions: Use the map below to answer questions 1 and 2.

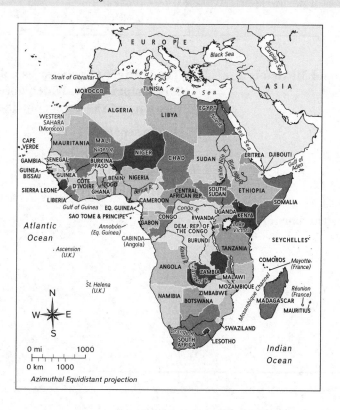

1 Which two physical boundaries separate Europe and Asia and from Africa?

A Atlantic Ocean and Indian Ocean

B Mediterranean Sea and Red Sea

C Red Sea and Indian Ocean

D Nile River and Mediterranean Sea

2 What physical feature makes up more than half of the border between Uganda and Tanzania?

A Lake Victoria

B The Red Sea

C The Nile River

D Lake Tanganyika

Directions: Use the map below to help answer questions 3 through 5.

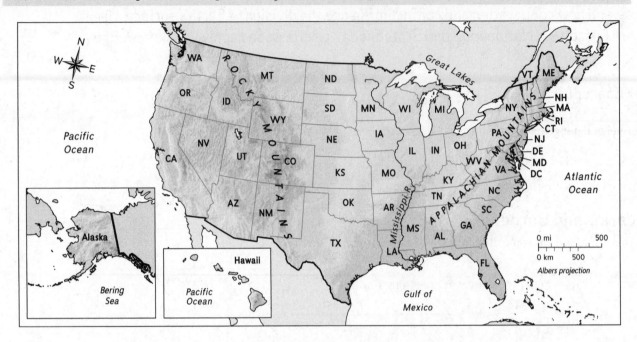

3 The border between Texas and Mexico is a political boundary and a

   A line of longitude.

   B geometric border.

   C physical boundary.

   D parallel.

4 The Pacific Ocean serves as the border for how many American states?

   A Three

   B Four

   C Five

   D Six

5 The borders of ten states coincide at the Mississippi River. Which definition fits the meaning of the term <u>coincide</u>?

   A To separate

   B To occur together

   C To blend

   D To split apart

✓ Test-Taking Tip

When taking a test, you might see a detailed image that is associated with a question. When you see something like this on a test, it helps to read the question first to determine exactly what it is asking. Then look at the image with the purpose of gathering only the details that will help you answer the question.

Geometric Borders

Some borders that follow imaginary lines such as lines of longitude and latitude are called geometric borders.

Directions: Use the map to answer questions 6 through 9.

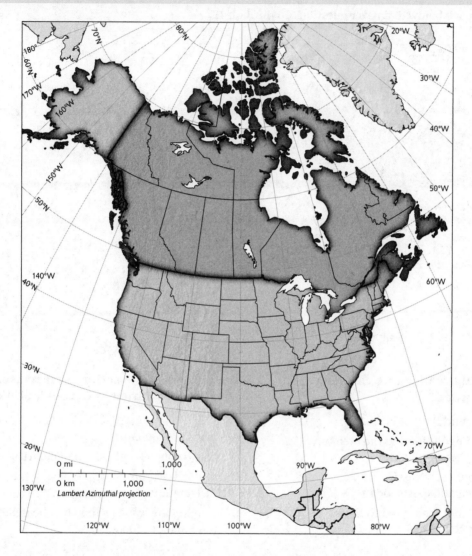

6 Which of the following lines of latitude pass through both the United States and Mexico?

A 20° N

B 30° N

C 40° N

D 50° N

7 Which of the following borders has both geometric and geographic portions?

A The border between the US and Mexico

B The border between Texas and Mexico

C The border between Canada and Greenland

D The border between Canada and Montana

8 Which of the following follows a line of longitude?

A The border between Alaska and Canada

B The western border of the United States

C The southern border of the United States

D The border between the United States and Canada

9 Lines of latitude increase in value

A from north to south.

B from south to north.

C further from the equator.

D closer to the equator.

The Creation of Borders

People create borders that separate ethnic and national groups, sometimes through war and sometimes through negotiations.

Directions: Use the maps below to answer questions 10 through 12.

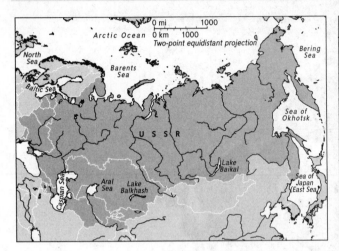

10 The two maps above illustrate changing borders as a result of

   A World Wars I and II.

   B the Russian Revolution and the breakup of the Soviet Union in 1991.

   C an alliance between Russia and its neighbors that still exists today.

   D negotiations that the United Nations conducted in the 1990s.

11 The fact that Kazakhstan has separate boundaries in the second map indicates that it has become a(n)

   A independent nation.

   B colony.

   C isolated region.

   D physical boundary.

12 The borders of the nations that reemerged after the dissolution of the Soviet Union were likely

   A won through battle.

   B based solely on physical boundaries.

   C drawn by a third party to ensure fair distribution of resources.

   D roughly the same as they had been before the Soviet Union.

13 Following the dissolution of the Soviet Union, Russia continued to have the same border with what nation?

   A Ukraine

   B Estonia

   C Mongolia

   D China

This lesson will help you discuss the effects of population growth and economic development, explain carrying capacity and global warming, define sustainability, and give examples of sustainable development. Use it with Core Lesson 9.3 *Human Activity and the Environment* to reinforce and apply your knowledge.

Key Concept

Economic development and a growing population are affecting the environment on Earth. Many people want to enact new policies to preserve Earth's natural resources.

Population Growth and Economic Development

As Earth's population continues to rise and as more and more of its natural resources are being used, many people are concerned about how these changes will affect our environment.

Directions: Questions 1 through 4 are based on the information below.

Since taking office, I have supported an all-of-the-above energy approach that will allow us to take control of our energy future, one where we safely and responsibly develop America's many energy resources—including natural gas, wind, solar, oil, clean coal, and biofuels—while investing in clean energy and increasing fuel efficiency standards to reduce our dependence on foreign oil.

. . . I have made the largest investment in clean energy and energy efficiency in American history and proposed an ambitious Clean Energy Standard to generate 80 percent of our electricity from clean energy sources like wind, solar, clean coal, and natural gas by 2035.

—President Barack Obama

1 President Obama's main concern seems to be developing more energy sources that are

A nonrenewable.

B profitable.

C renewable.

D expensive.

2 Which of the following best explains why President Obama would take an "all-of-the-above" approach to finding energy sources?

A Without new sources, the United States might exceed its carrying capacity.

B The president needs to be careful not to alienate any voting group.

C The United States does not have enough of any one particular source of energy.

D Some citizens refuse to use certain types of energy sources.

3 By setting a goal of generating 80 percent of electricity from clean energy sources, President Obama is trying to promote

A carrying capacity.

B sustainable development.

C foreign competition.

D the greenhouse effect.

4 Which of the "clean energy" sources listed by President Obama are nonrenewable resources?

A Clean coal and natural gas

B Wind power and clean coal

C Solar power and natural gas

D Wind power and clean coal

Global Warming and Climate Change

Carbon dioxide is one of many gases that cause Earth's greenhouse effect, or its ability to prevent some heat from the Sun from escaping back into space. Without the greenhouse effect, Earth would be too cold for life.

Directions: Questions 5 and 6 are based on the information below.

Francisco Estrada is an ecological economist at the Free University in Amsterdam. He studied temperature data from 1850 to 2010 to determine whether there was a correlation between fossil fuel emissions and global warming. Here is some of what he found:

"A cooling period between 1940 and 1970 had previously been chalked up to natural variability and the Sun-shielding effect of pollution emitted by European industries, as they recovered after the Second World War. But Estrada and his colleagues found that it followed a reduction in greenhouse-gas emissions associated with economic downturns, when industries were less active. Significant drops in emissions occurred during the First World War, the Great Depression of the 1930s and the Second World War."

—Hannah Hoag, *Nature*, November 10, 2013

5 **What does Estrada now believe caused the cooling period between 1940 and 1970?**

A A decrease in greenhouse gas emissions because of a decrease in the Sun-shielding effect of pollution

B An increase in greenhouse gas emissions because of a decrease in the Sun-shielding effect of pollution

C A decrease in greenhouse gas emissions because industries were less active

D An increase in greenhouse gas emissions because of the economic downturn

6 **From the passage, you can infer that business owners might argue that**

A burning fossil fuels is not a cost-effective way to produce energy.

B curbing greenhouse gas emissions would harm the economy.

C human activity contributes to global warming and should be examined.

D burning fossil fuels pollutes the environment and should be curbed.

Directions: Answer the following questions.

7 **One effect of climate change is that**

A water availability is changing.

B the Poles are becoming colder.

C fossil fuels are being completely depleted.

D water is receding in coastal areas.

8 **Which of the following is a fossil fuel?**

A Carbon dioxide

B Nuclear energy

C Natural gas

D Quartz

Sustainability

Sustainability is a term that refers to living within limits when it comes to the use of natural resources.

Directions: Answer the following questions.

9 Sustainable development is partially in response to a reduction in resources, and also to what environmental trend?

   A   Changing rainfall patterns

   B   Decreasing biodiversity

   C   Industrial pollution

   D   The greenhouse effect

10 One way to support sustainable development would be to

   A   call for higher emissions standards.

   B   oppose development of hydroelectric power.

   C   advocate for more public and less private transportation.

   D   pressure oil companies to avoid oil spills.

11 In addition to the size and growth of Earth's human population, which of the following is a reason why Earth's natural resources are being depleted?

   A   Natural resources are becoming more costly to produce and distribute.

   B   Higher standards of living are allowing more people to use more resources.

   C   Decreased access to resources is leading to wasteful consumption.

   D   People are destroying resources to protest their unequal distribution.

12 Countries such as China, which have high populations and growing economies, most likely

   A   are contributing more toward climate change.

   B   will not have to endure the effects of climate change.

   C   cannot control their dependence on natural resources.

   D   will have a harder time promoting sustainable development.

13 The production of automobiles with higher fuel efficiency is most dependent on

   A   government regulation.

   B   government subsidies.

   C   consumer demand.

   D   technology.

14 Warmer temperatures worldwide can lead to

   A   overproduction of food crops.

   B   fewer hurricanes.

   C   greater cloud cover in tropical regions.

   D   higher ocean levels.

Directions: Questions 15 through 18 are based on the graph below.

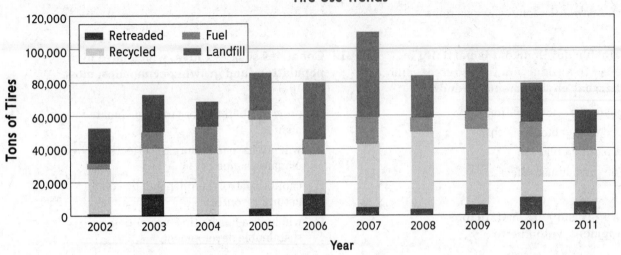

Source: http://www.ecy.wa.gov/programs/swfa/tires/reuse.html

15 **How does the graph illustrate the concept of sustainable development?**

   A It shows that the amount of tires used as fuel has decreased.

   B It shows that retreaded tires are the smallest portion of tires each year.

   C It shows how many natural resources are being used to make new tires.

   D It shows the amount of tires being reused and recycled.

16 **Which tire use was the largest in eight of the ten years represented in this graph?**

   A Retreaded

   B Recycled

   C Fuel

   D Landfill

17 **Which year shows the most sustainability for tires?**

   A 2011

   B 2007

   C 2005

   D 2003

18 **Which of the following events might cause the number of reused or recycled tires to decline?**

   A A rise in safety concerns about retreaded tires

   B A ban on tires in landfills

   C The adoption of shredded-tire playground surfaces by more school systems

   D The development of an improved process for turning used tires into fuel

 Test-Taking Tip

When you are answering questions about a graph, study the graph first to see any patterns or trends that the graph reveals.

This lesson will help you understand that natural resources are distributed and utilized in various ways, recognize the many ecosystems on Earth, and consider weather and climate systems. Use it with Core Lesson 10.1 *Concepts of Region and Place* to reinforce and apply your knowledge.

Key Concept

The planet Earth is made of many interconnected physical systems, including land, water, plants, animals, and weather.

Earth's Structure and Regions

The surface of Earth is composed of vast oceans as well as large landmasses with mountains, hills, valleys, and plains.

Directions: Questions 1 through 3 are based on the image of Earth below.

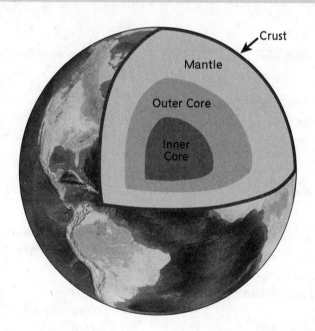

1 All living organisms on Earth live on the layer known as the

A crust.

B mantle.

C continent.

D ocean.

2 The difference between the inner and outer core can best be described as the difference between

A land and water.

B gas and solid.

C liquid and solid.

D heat and cold.

3 The thickest layer shown in this graphic is made of

A solid rock.

B liquid metal.

C hot gas.

D solid metal.

Directions: Questions 4 and 5 are based on the graph below.

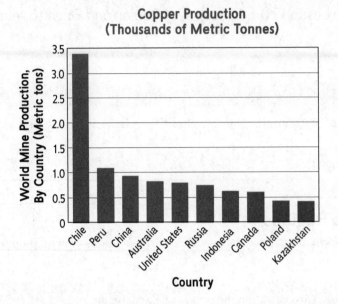

Copper Production
(Thousands of Metric Tonnes)

Source: http://www.indexmundi.com/minerals/?product=copper&graph=production

4 **Chile produces more copper than the**

  A rest of the world combined.

  B next three-highest producers combined.

  C next six-highest producers combined.

  D world can use at this time.

5 **Which two continents lead the world in copper production?**

  A Asia and Africa

  B Australia and Europe

  C North and South America

  D Asia and Europe

Directions: Answer the following questions.

6 **An isthmus is defined as**

  A a piece of land that is completely surrounded by water.

  B a narrow strip of land that projects into a large body of water.

  C a strip of land with sea on either side, connecting two larger land areas.

  D an area on or near the sea or ocean.

7 **The customs, beliefs, practices, and language shared by a people who live in a region together make up its**

  A culture.

  B human resources.

  C ecosystem.

  D factors of production.

Ecosystems

An ecosystem is a community of organisms in an area and the natural resources with which the community interacts.

Directions: Answer the questions below.

8 **Unlike land ecosystems, marine ecosystems can be affected by**

    A   temperature.

    B   climate.

    C   amount of sunlight.

    D   salt concentration.

9 **Flowering plants, shrubs, coyotes, ground-nesting birds, and prairie dogs are found in which ecosystem?**

    A   Grassland

    B   Desert

    C   Forest

    D   Tundra

10 **Both tundra and boreal forest ecosystems**

    A   are found on the continent of Africa.

    B   depend on high amounts of sunlight.

    C   have drastic seasonal temperature changes.

    D   are very cold for most of the year.

11 **How does a biome differ from an ecosystem?**

    A   An ecosystem occurs on land, and a biome occurs in water.

    B   Many similar ecosystems in one region make up a biome.

    C   Ecosystems are defined by climate, but biomes are defined by plant and animals species.

    D   An ecosystem is an area that contains many unrelated biomes.

12 **What continent is home to only one biome?**

    A   Australia

    B   Africa

    C   Antarctica

    D   South America

13 **The two broad categories of biomes are**

    A   polar and tropical.

    B   terrestrial and aquatic.

    C   northern and southern.

    D   warm and cool.

✔ Test-Taking Tip

Note how much time you are given to complete a test. Keep an eye on the time as you are taking the test. Stop periodically to make sure that you are on target to finish. Plan ahead so you have time at the end of the exam to review your answers. Make sure that you have answered all the questions and have not made any errors.

Weather and Climate

Weather changes daily, but climate is determined by the weather patterns that an area experiences over a long period of time.

Directions: Use the map below to help answer questions 14 through 17.

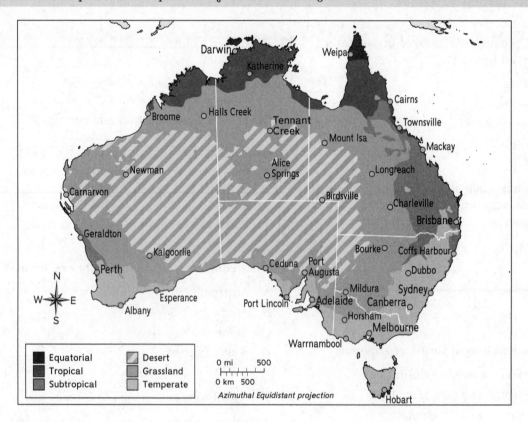

14 **Because Australia is below the Equator, the tropical climate in the country is**

A along the west coast.

B in the North.

C in the Southeast.

D extremely small.

15 **Australia's five major population centers are Sydney, Melbourne, Brisbane, Perth, and Adelaide. Based on the map, why might these cities appeal to so many people?**

A Westerly winds keep the cities cool in the summer.

B The ocean and distance from the Equator moderate the climate.

C The elevation and distance from the Equator ensure cool summers.

D Proximity to grasslands has allowed the cities to expand.

16 **Australia's large desert climate**

A is more than 1,600 km wide.

B is half the size of the entire country.

C is by a subtropical climate.

D has no human habitation.

17 **Of the following cities, which is most likely to receive large amounts of annual rainfall?**

A Weipa

B Alice Springs

C Broome

D Hobart

This lesson will help you understand the diversity of physical geography and human geography and how landforms affect human settlement. Use it with Core Lesson 10.2 *Natural and Cultural Diversity* to reinforce and apply your knowledge.

Key Concept

Earth is rich in physical and cultural diversity, as seen by its landscapes and its people.

Physical Diversity

The landscapes of Earth exhibit vast diversity—from flat plains to rugged mountains and from wetlands and rivers to dry prairies and deserts.

Directions: Use the map below to help answer questions 1 and 2.

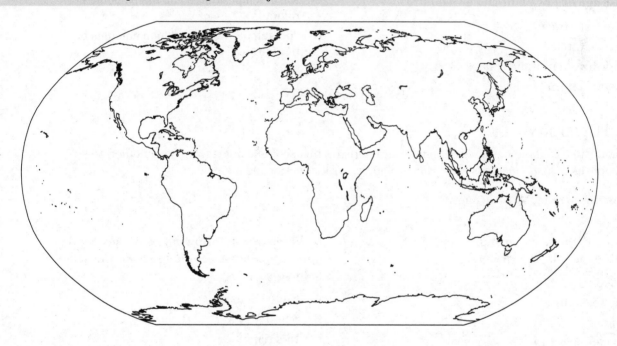

1 Which of these continents is the smallest?

  A South America

  B Europe

  C North America

  D Australia

2 Earth's five oceans are the Atlantic, Pacific,

  A Indian, Mediterranean, and Arctic.

  B Arctic, Arabian, and Northern.

  C Southern, Arctic, and Indian.

  D Mediterranean, Southern, and Indian.

Directions: Read the following questions. Then select the correct answers.

3 Climate zones are determined by a region's characteristics such as latitude or distance from the Equator, nearness to a large body of water, air currents and landforms. In which of the following locations might you expect to find an arid, desert-type climate?

A   Sixty degrees north latitude

B   Near the Equator and bordered by the Pacific Ocean

C   Interior of Australia surrounded by mountains

D   Northeast coast of China

4 Which location is most likely to have the lowest density of plant and animal life?

A   Central Africa

B   Arctic Circle

C   Northwestern United States

D   Southeastern Europe

5 Which definition best fits the meaning of the term "diversity"?

A   Cultural relevance

B   Ability to adapt

C   Distinctiveness

D   Variety

6 Plant and animal diversity and density are greatest in environments with

A   warm temperatures and low amounts of rainfall.

B   cool temperatures and low amounts of rainfall.

C   warm temperatures and high amounts of rainfall.

D   cool temperatures and high amounts of rainfall.

Cultural Diversity

Just as Earth's physical regions have defining characteristics that set them apart from one another, so do Earth's people have languages, customs, values, and beliefs that define them.

Directions: Answer the following questions.

7 Language, food, art, customs, and clothing are all elements of a group's

A   race.

B   nationality.

C   culture.

D   family structure.

8 Countries such as the United States and Nigeria that have many cultures within different regions are called

A   homogenous.

B   multicultural.

C   traditional.

D   biomes.

9 In which of the following countries would you expect most people to speak the same language?

A   United States

B   South Africa

C   Nigeria

D   Japan

10 Sanskrit, Armenian, German, Italian, and Spanish are all part of what language grouping?

A   Indo-European

B   Latin

C   Indo-Aryan

D   Gallic

Directions: Use the chart below to help answer questions 11 and 12.

Fifteen Largest Ancestries: 2000

In millions, percentage of total population in parentheses.

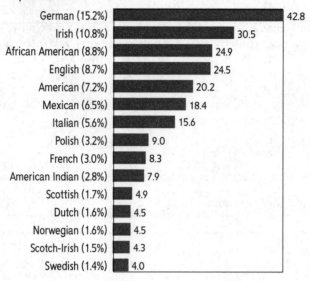

German (15.2%) 42.8
Irish (10.8%) 30.5
African American (8.8%) 24.9
English (8.7%) 24.5
American (7.2%) 20.2
Mexican (6.5%) 18.4
Italian (5.6%) 15.6
Polish (3.2%) 9.0
French (3.0%) 8.3
American Indian (2.8%) 7.9
Scottish (1.7%) 4.9
Dutch (1.6%) 4.5
Norwegian (1.6%) 4.5
Scotch-Irish (1.5%) 4.3
Swedish (1.4%) 4.0

Source: U.S. Census Bureau, Census 2000 special tabulation.

11 The United States is ethnically diverse. The high number of German, Irish, African American, and English people is largely because

   A more recent immigrants came from these areas.

   B these groups tend to have more children than other groups.

   C these groups tend to live longer than other groups.

   D these groups came very early and have more descendants than other groups.

12 Why will charts like this become less accurate over time?

   A The Census Bureau is becoming less important.

   B More people will have diverse, multicultural ancestries.

   C The numbers will get too large to track accurately.

   D Some ethnic groups will grow faster than others.

✓ Test-Taking Tip

When you are answering a question related to a chart with a lot of data, read the question first so you can target the specific data in the chart needed to answer the question.

Landforms and Human Settlement

Physical factors such as landforms, climate, and environment affect where people choose to settle and how their culture develops.

Directions: Answer the following questions.

13 The Lakota people lived on the Great Plains of North America. As a consequence, their diet most likely included

A   fish.

B   bison.

C   bear meat.

D   waterfowl.

14 The increasing movement of people and businesses into outlying areas around cities is often called

A   emigration.

B   urban sprawl.

C   forced migration.

D   suburban expansion.

Directions: Use the map below to help answer questions 15 and 16.

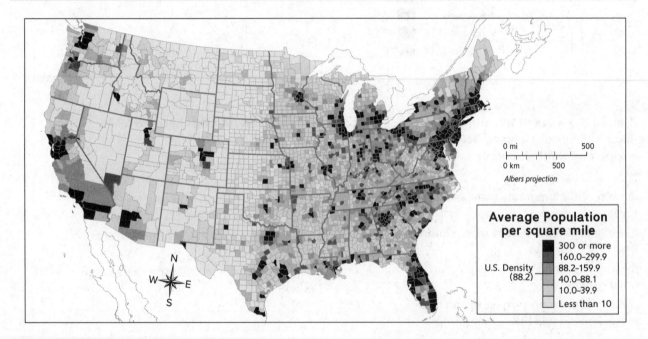

15 The large populations of California, Michigan, Ohio, Pennsylvania, Florida, and New York are best explained by the observation that

A   people generally prefer to live near large bodies of water.

B   the climate of these states is temperate.

C   these states have more natural resources.

D   immigrants are unevenly distributed across the country.

16 The states on this map with the lowest population density are grouped in which quadrant of the United States?

A   Northeast

B   Northwest

C   Southeast

D   Southwest

This lesson will help you understand what is meant by the study of demography; recognize that population growth, migrations, and settlement patterns tell a great deal about how humans interact with their environment; and explain the general trend toward urban growth in the United States. Use it with Core Lesson 10.3 *Population Trends and Issues* to reinforce and apply your knowledge.

▌Key Concept

Humans interact with Earth by moving from place to place, building new communities, and expanding their populations.

Demography

The statistical study of the size, growth, movement, and distribution of people is called demography. Governments and other institutions rely on demographic information to forecast and plan the future.

Directions: Use the map below to answer questions 1 and 2.

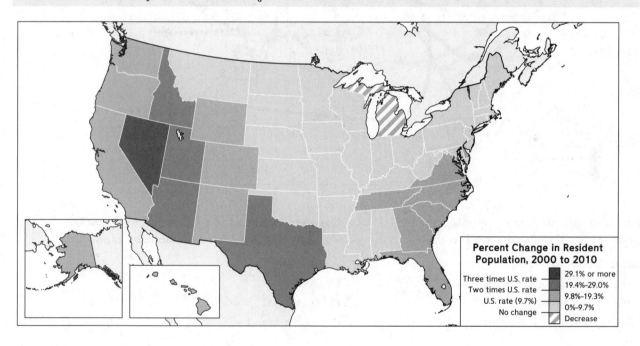

Percent Change in Resident Population, 2000 to 2010

Three times U.S. rate	29.1% or more
Two times U.S. rate	19.4%–29.0%
U.S. rate (9.7%)	9.8%–19.3%
No change	0%–9.7%
	Decrease

1 According to the information given in this graphic, new government services might be needed in the

   A southeast.

   B northeast.

   C northcentral

   D southwest.

2 Which state had the lowest growth rate in its population?

   A Pennsylvania

   B Tennessee

   C Arizona

   D Nevada

Directions: Answer the following questions.

3   **Which of the following situations best indicates a growing population?**

A   Low fertility and low mortality rates

B   High fertility and high mortality rates

C   Low fertility and high mortality rates

D   High fertility and low mortality rates

4   **The main reason the government uses census data is to determine**

A   how much each person should be taxed.

B   where citizens should move in the future.

C   where new services might be needed.

D   which states are the most successful.

Migration and Population

Migration, the movement of people from one place to another, can occur for a number of different reasons.

Directions: Use the migration map below to help answer questions 5 through 7.

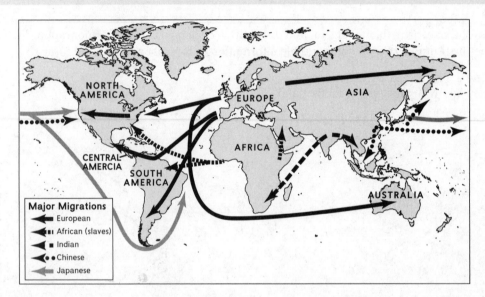

5   **As shown on the map, most people who emigrated from Japan migrated to**

A   Australia and East Asia.

B   North America and South America.

C   Africa and South Asia.

D   Europe and South Africa.

6   **According to the map, which of the following groups continued their migration across the United States?**

A   Europeans

B   Africans

C   Asians

D   Chinese

7   **Europeans migrated to several continents by ship, and to which continent by land?**

A   Africa

B   Asia

C   Australia

D   North America

Urban Growth

The last two centuries witnessed a trend toward the movement of people from rural, agricultural areas to urban areas, or cities. More recently, people have been moving from the cities to the suburbs.

Directions: Use the map below to answer questions 8 through 10.

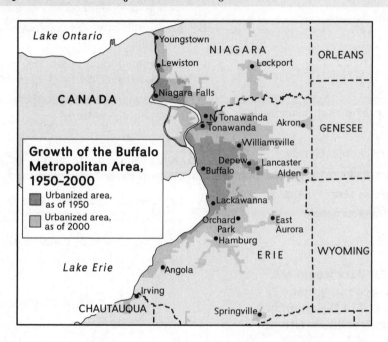

Growth of the Buffalo Metropolitan Area, 1950–2000
- Urbanized area, as of 1950
- Urbanized area, as of 2000

8 Buffalo, New York, may fit the description of "urban sprawl" because

  A the city population declined, while the metropolitan area has expanded.

  B more people today live near the center of the city.

  C many farmers have moved from Niagara County to the city limits.

  D the city continues to incorporate smaller towns into its governed area.

9 Which two counties have experienced significant population growth?

  A Ontario and Wyoming

  B Chautauqua and Orleans

  C Erie and Niagara

  D Lancaster and Orchard Park

10 East Aurora is an example of what kind of urban growth?

  A Forced migration

  B Inner city growth

  C Rural town growth

  D Urban sprawl

11 Which geographic features prevent the uniform outward growth of population from Buffalo?

  A The Canadian border and Lake Erie

  B Lake Erie and Lake Ontario

  C The Canadian border and the Niagara County border

  D Lake Erie and the Niagara County border

✔ Test-Taking Tip

You can understand a map by reading the title and looking at the map key to determine the information that the map is conveying.

Directions: Answer the following questions.

12 Based on what you know about urban migration, what period of population movement is characterized by urban sprawl?

    A 1800–1850

    B 1870–1950

    C 1950–1980

    D 1980–2010

13 "Cultural diffusion" is a term that describes the

    A loss of cultural traits as people migrate.

    B saving of cultural traits in distinct regions.

    C change of cultural traits as people migrate.

    D spreading of cultural traits as people migrate.

14 Which set of demographic data would tell government officials in a country that improvements were needed in the country's health care system or with child nutrition?

    A High birthrate

    B High fertility rate

    C High death rate

    D High infant mortality rate

15 Which is an example of how a group of people became refugees?

    A The establishment of the nation of Israel on land also claimed by Palestinians

    B Migrations after the collapse of the Greek economy

    C Suburban population increases due to rising urban crime rates

    D The slave trade in the sixteenth and seventeenth centuries

16 If the economic performance of a country is improving, then

    A its standard of living is dropping.

    B its standard of living is improving.

    C its gross domestic product is down.

    D its per capita income is shrinking.

Lesson 1.1

Types of Modern and Historical Governments, p. 1

1. **A** In an autocracy, all power is held by a single person.

2. **B** Both the United States Congress and the Canadian Parliament are made up of representatives who are elected by the citizens of their respective countries.

3. **A** In a constitutional monarchy, monarchs have ceremonial power, whereas dictators have absolute power.

4. **C** An oligarchy is a system involving rule by a small group of people.

5. **D** Both Aristotle and de Tocqueville are concerned that people have equal power, regardless of their financial means.

6. **B** Aristotle believed that when government was in the hands of the rich, whether they were many or few, that government was an oligarchy.

7. **D** de Tocqueville was concerned that democracy would respect the rights of both capitalists and citizens.

8. **B** Direct democracies, in which all citizens have a direct say in every issue, are only workable on a small scale, for example in a New England town.

9. **A** Both documents state that government is instituted to safeguard the rights of the people and that just power is derived from the consent of the people.

10. **C** The authors wanted the Constitution to be able to adapt as the nation changed and grew.

11. **D** The third amendment prohibits a specific practice that was loathed by colonists during colonial times.

12. **A** The first ten amendments are known as the Bill of Rights.

13. **B** The Fifteenth Amendment extends the right to vote to African American men, but women, regardless of race, were only allowed to vote upon passage of the Nineteenth Amendment.

14. **D** The Twenty-Sixth Amendment set the voting age for state and federal elections at eighteen.

15. **C** The Twenty-Fourth Amendment made unconstitutional the practice of requiring voters to pay a poll tax before they could vote.

16. **C** A democracy is a form of government in which the people, or the governed, rule.

17. **B** The purpose of both the Bill of Rights and the Magna Carta was to protect individual rights and limit the power of government.

Lesson 1.2

American Constitutional Democracy, p. 5

1. **D** The Framers of the Articles of Confederation most likely reacted to their experience with British colonial rule.

2. **B** A government based on a constitution holds only those powers granted in its constitution.

3. **B** Courts and tax collectors seized farms as repayment of debt and taxes, leading farmers to attack courts and to raid state arsenals for weapons.

4. **D** Natural rights include the basic human rights that should be granted to all people and not taken away.

5. **C** Citizens hold the power in a government by electing their own representatives at all levels of government.

6. **A** The executive branch exercises checks and balances on the legislative and judicial branches by holding the power to nominate federal judges.

7. **B** By creating three branches of government with separate roles and responsibilities, the people had less fear of being too strictly governed by a leader or small group of leaders.

8 **C** The judicial branch determines the constitutionality of laws currently in existence.

9. **B** Federalism is the concept of a system of government in which power is shared between federal, or national government, and local government.

10. **C** All states have 2 Senate seats, regardless of state size or population.

11. **D** All of the original 13 states eventually ratified the constitution.

12. **C** A faction is a smaller group of people who hold different views, which they make clear to the larger group.

13. **A** Madison believed that freedom (liberty) would not need to be limited, because the freedom exercised by many other groups would be enough to keep a faction from taking control.

14. **B** The Bill of Rights consists of the first ten amendments to the Constitution.

15. **C** The enforcement of the nation's laws is directed by the executive branch.

16. **A** The rule of law means that the law is preeminent over any other factor, including any leader, group, or concern.

17. **D** The colonists wanted to be sure that the rights that were violated by the British before and during the war—freedom of speech and the press, the right to bear arms, the right against illegal searches and seizures, for example—would be addressed in the new constitution.

18. **A** An amendment must be proposed by Congress and then ratified by a three-fourths majority of the states.

19. **C** New amendments to the Constitution ensure that it is connected to current issues as they occur.

20. **D** Forty-nine percent of those polled were in favor of passing stronger gun laws, while fifty percent were opposed, indicating that Americans are evenly divided on the issue of stronger gun laws.

Lesson 1.3

Structure of American Government, p. 9

1. **C** The president's chief job is to run the executive department.

2. **C** The checks and balances written into the Constitution, which allow each branch of government (executive, legislative, judicial) to "check" or prevent the others from becoming too powerful, includes the power of Congress to amend a law found unconstitutional by the Supreme Court.

3. **C** Though Congress's primary duty is to write legislation, other duties include representing the interests of their constituents and overseeing the federal budget.

4. **A** The legislative branch can override a presidential veto.

5. **B** The president and Congress share military powers.

6. **A** The executive branch is in charge of negotiations with other countries.

7. **A** The president can use television, radio, and the Internet to appeal directly to the public, going over the heads of Congress to make his case.

8. **C** The author implies that less media reach and a different notion of the role of the president meant that before the 20th century, presidents did not have as much influence on the legislative process.

9. **C** The growth of social media has further expanded the media available to members of government for contact with citizens.

10. **D** The power to levy taxes, hold elections, and borrow money belongs to both the state and federal governments, but the power to establish schools belongs only to the state governments.

11. **A** Powers that are not specifically claimed by the federal government in the Constitution are held by states.

12. **C** The federal government set up the bank to control the amount of unregulated currency issued by state banks, which falls under their duty to coin money and regulate its value.

13. **B** This is an example of a concurrent power, held by both the state and the federal government.

14. **D** By allowing the states to tax the federal government, the states could use that power to weaken federal banks and other services, giving states unintended power to control certain aspects of the federal government.

15. **C** Direct initiative gives citizens of a state power to directly influence legislation in their state by submitting legislation for the legislature to consider.

16. **C** A referendum is a way for citizens to have an issue considered through voting.

17. **A** Nebraska is the only state with one legislative body rather than two.

18. **D** The lieutenant governor, like the vice president, presides over the legislature and replaces the governor if he or she dies, resigns, or is removed from office.

19. **A** The referendum process allows citizens to collect signatures to get a new law created.

Lesson 2.1

Individual Rights and Responsibilities, p. 13

1. **B** Mason's ideas regarding due process were expressed in the Sixth Amendment.

2. **A** To be impartial is to be unbiased.

3. **A** The right to a fair and speedy trial is guaranteed in the Bill of Rights.

4. **B** The Establishment Clause prevents the government from establishing or supporting any religion.

5. **C** To prohibit is to prevent.

6. **C** The right against self-incrimination described in this ruling is protected by the Fifth Amendment.

7. **B** Indigent means to be unable to afford.

8. **C** In 1896 the Supreme Court ruled that segregation was legal under the "separate but equal" doctrine.

9. **D** The Supreme Court ruling allowed "separate but equal" facilities, leading to Jim Crow laws that separated the races in public places.

10. **C** Dr. King's views are most clearly reflected in the Supreme Court's decision in *Brown* v. *Board of Education, Topeka, Kansas,* which declared segregation in public facilities unconstitutional.

11. **B** Sojourner Truth's famous speech argued that as a woman she was as strong and able as a man, proven by her strengths and experiences. She stood as an example of the strength of all women.

12. **B** Sojourner Truth was an abolitionist as well as a women's rights advocate.

13. **D** The Equal Pay Act of 1963, which made it illegal to pay men more than women for the same job, was passed after women gained the right to vote in national elections, but before it was illegal to discriminate against women in hiring.

14. **C** During and after World War II, working women found that they were not paid the same as men, were not able to get the same kinds of jobs as men, and were often given jobs that did not allow them to advance.

15. **B** Suffrage is the right to vote in a political election.

Lesson 2.2

Political Parties, Campaigns, and Elections, p. 17

1. **C** By identifying issues and concerns that were shared by different types of Americans, Senator Obama was most likely trying to appeal to independent voters.

2. **A** Senator Obama's speech helped outline his party's beliefs, a task that is one of a national convention's main goals.

3. **C** Third-party candidates often deal with an issue or a set of issues that some voters believe the major parties are not adequately addressing.

4. **A** Political parties, even lesser known third parties, provide candidates with a label and a set of shared values and goals that help identify the candidate and what they stand for.

5. **D** The nature of the two-party system means that the Democratic and Republican parties wield more power and have more money, both of which influence the outcome of elections.

6. **D** In American political cartoons, the elephant symbolizes the Republican party, so Roosevelt pushing an elephant with a load bearing the words *Panama Canal Project* symbolizes the president's push to convince Republicans to back that project.

7. **C** Political cartoons combine symbols and caricatures to convey a specific message.

8. **C** Television and print ads, as well as offices and staff, cost a lot of money to fund.

9. **B** The electoral vote, which determines the outcome of presidential elections, is determined by electors of each state, whereas the popular vote is the total number of votes cast for a presidential candidate.

10. **B** Because Bush won Florida, all of the states electoral votes were awarded to him, even though he did not win the popular vote.

11. **B** A lobbyist works for an interest group in swaying public officials toward policies that benefit the interest group.

12. **D** Because they charge high fees for their services, lobbyists give wealthy individuals and groups more influence over the legislative process.

Lesson 2.3

Structure of American Government, p. 21

1. **C** As it is used in this context, "domestic" refers to things that happen within one's own country.

2. **C** Posterity refers to future generations.

3. **B** The Preamble affirms that the power of the government comes from the people.

4. **C** The purpose of federal government policies is to set out laws and guidelines that address problems and issues that affect everyone in the nation.

5. **B** The rules and guidelines of an individual school would be considered school policy. While those rules may be current, Answer C is not the best way to classify them. Answer A refers to policies that affect a wider span of people. Answer D is a subset of school and public policy.

6. **C** Public policies affect everyone in society. The sales tax rate is a state policy that affects everyone in the state. The other options are personal decisions.

7. **B** Once Congress passes a new policy or the president signs an order for a new policy, it is up to government agencies to implement the policy.

8. **A** While weight limits falls under transportation policy, emissions falls under environmental policy, and medical liability coverage falls under healthcare policy, the seatbelt requirement is a public safety policy.

9. **D** Selective service affects everyone in the nation, so it is an example of federal policy. Answers A, B, and C are levels of government that would impact only the people living in that area.

10. **D** Since the final step in the public policy process involves evaluating the effectiveness of the policy, public policy is always in the process of being reshaped and refined.

11. **A** Congress adopts a policy if a majority in Congress votes in favor of the policy.

12. **D** The next step in the process after implementation of a policy is the evaluation of the results.

13. **B** Lobbying is a process by which individuals and interest groups can influence the lawmaking process.

14. **D** According to this ruling, direct personal contact, such as buying lunch or dinner for government officials, can threaten the democratic process.

15. **C** Citizens can indirectly influence public policy by exerting pressure on Congress.

16. **C** Special interest groups are organized around specific issues, such as preventing texting while driving, while public interest groups work for changes in public policy, and economic interest groups focus on business policy.

Lesson 3.1

American Revolution, p. 25

1. **C** The Mayflower Compact was a written agreement that set out the rules by which the Pilgrims would govern themselves.

2. **C** Both groups had strict religious convictions and founded colonies based on these convictions.

3. **B** This document is an example of a charter, or a written code of rules.

4. **D** A colony is a land controlled by another nation.

5. **A** Dickinson, like many colonists, opposed the Townshend Acts because they levied taxes on the colonists, who were not represented in the British Parliament.

6. **D** Many colonists responded to these taxes by refusing to buy the taxed goods.

7. **D** As a result of the Boston Tea Party, parliament passed the Coercive Acts to punish Boston

8. **B** Since this passage asks the king to maintain peace and help his subject—that is, the colonists—we can conclude that it is taken from the Olive Branch Petition.

9. **D** The Olive Branch Petition was an attempt to make peace.

10. **B** The British victory over the French and the resulting need to defend additional territory increased expenses of the British government, which was badly in debt. The British determined that the colonists would share some of the cost. Answer C states part of the British problem but does not address its actions, which are key to the paragraph. Answer D states two results of the British decision.

11. **A** This sentence states the problem that the British faced after the war—the cause. It also states the new policy that was the response to that problem—the effect.

12. **B** The Great Compromise made population the basis of representation in the House, but each state had an equal vote in the Senate.

13. **D** The Stamp Act imposed a new tax on the colonists by the British Parliament, where the colonists had no representatives. Answers A, B, and C, are other rights that were expressed during the formation of the new country.

14. **C** Money was borrowed to carry on the Revolutionary War and Congress had no means to raise the funds to pay back that debt. Answer A is incorrect; the Congress did print money. Answer B is

incorrect; Congress had no plan to build roads. Answer D is incorrect; the statement is true but was not a reason that the federal government was weak under the Articles of Confederation.

15. **C**   The Articles of Confederation provided for a unicameral legislature, whereas the Constitution provides for a bicameral legislature: the Senate and the House of Representatives.

16. **D**   The Virginia Plan gave every state an equal vote in the federal legislature, while the Great Compromise provided that each state had an equal vote in the Senate but that representation in the House was dictated by population. Answers A and C describe powers of Congress under the Articles of Confederation but not under either the Virginia Plan or the Great Compromise. Answer B was part of the Virginia Plan, but was unchanged by the Great Compromise.

Lesson 3.2

A New Nation, p. 29

1. **D**   The Northwest Ordinance of 1787 established the process by which new states could be added to the Union.

2. **B**   A township is defined as an area of land that is controlled by a government.

3. **C**   The Land Ordinance of 1785 made land available for $1.00 per acre, attracting thousands of settlers and leading to the admission of five states.

4. **D**   The Lewis and Clark Expedition provided essential information about the new territory.

5. **C**   All of these offices were originally appointed by President Washington.

6. **B**   Jay's Treaty did not settle all the issues the United States had with Great Britain.

7. **B**   As a strict constructionist, Jefferson would not have proceeded with any activity that was not specifically given to him in the Constitution.

8. **B**   Jefferson pushed past his own concerns in order to provide for a growing nation, both in land and natural resources.

9. **C**   Clay of Kentucky and Calhoun of South Carolina were elected in 1810 and helped persuade Congress to declare war in 1812.

10. **C**   In the period immediately before the War of 1812, Americans were angry that the French and British kept impressing American sailors to serve on their ships. Answers A, B, and D were all issues that were resolved a decade earlier.

11. **B**   The boundaries agreed to in the Treaty of Paris created a large nation. Answer A is also true, but it is not the reason the treaty was favorable to the US. Answers C and D were achieved by other ordinances.

12. **B**   In December 1814, two weeks before the Battle of New Orleans, the Treaty of Ghent was signed, ending the war.

13. **A**   One of the positive outcomes of winning the War of 1812 was a strong feeling of American nationalism.

14. **D**   Manifest Destiny was the belief that Americans were destined to settle all of North America from the Atlantic Ocean to the Pacific Ocean.

15. **C**   The concept of Manifest Destiny drove the United States to acquire new territories; the United States annexed Texas in 1848.

16. **C**   When the Cherokees brought suit against the state of Georgia, the Supreme Court ruled in their favor, but Jackson refused to enforce its decision.

Lesson 3.3

Civil War and Reconstruction, p. 33

1. **B** Under the triangular trade, traders brought sugar and molasses from the West Indies to the colonies to make rum, which was shipped to Africa in exchange for enslaved people, who were taken back to the Caribbean and the colonies.

2. **C** Since the plantation system relied on slave labor, wealthy planters would be most likely to support the expansion of slavery.

3. **B** When white indentured servants ran away, they were difficult to recover, so new workers had to be trained.

4. **C** Rum was shipped from the colonies to Africa. Answers A, B, and D traveled along the other legs of the route.

5. **D** Since each state is represented by two Senators, the addition of a new slave state would upset the balance between free and slave states in the Senate.

6. **A** Maine was not a separate state at this time. It was part of Massachusetts and was included in the Massachusetts vote.

7. **B** To preserve the balance between slave and free states in the Senate, Maine was admitted to the Union at the same time as Missouri.

8. **B** The Missouri Compromise closed the area known as Unorganized Territory to slavery.

9. **B** When Lincoln gave his address, there were still some slave states that stayed in the Union, and Lincoln did not want to alienate them by attacking the slave states that had seceded.

10. **C** Lincoln used persuasive language to try to convince the Confederate states to re-join the Union.

11. **C** Lincoln had thought the war would be over quickly by taking Richmond, but Lee's army held back the North.

12. **A** Because many of the battles were fought in the South, the South had a familiarity with battlegrounds that the North did not have.

13. **D** By having ex-Confederates swear loyalty to the Union, Johnson hoped to prevent them from declaring war on the Union again.

14. **C** When it began, the primary goal of the Civil War was preserving the Union. As the Union experienced successes during the course of the war, Lincoln was able to promote his agenda of freeing the enslaved people.

15. **A** The Thirteenth Amendment abolished slavery in the United States.

16. **C** Southern governments instituted black codes to limit the rights of African Americans following the Civil War.

17. **D** By the 1870's, economic concerns had caused many Northerners to abandon the cause of Reconstruction and the problems that plagued African Americans.

18. **C** Indentured servitude was still permissible as punishment for a crime in which someone had been convicted.

Lesson 3.4

European Settlement and Population of the Americas, p. 37

1. **A** Anything that causes people to leave their native countries, such as economic hardship, is called a push factor.

2. B This statement includes an important detail of the section and abides by the other steps to follow when summarizing. Answer A is not an accurate statement. Answer C is a very specific detail that does not adhere to the steps for summarizing. Answer D is a statement of opinion, which does not belong in a summary.

3. B Those who could afford the train fare continued west in search of better jobs.

4. A While immigrants did introduce new ideas and techniques, their greatest contribution was the hard work they invested in helping American companies grow and prosper.

5. C Northern Europe, with more than 7,816,000 immigrants, was the source of the largest group of immigrants.

6. A Because of the large influx of Southern and Eastern Europeans during this period, cities in the northeast became overcrowded.

7. D Most Latin American immigrants during this period worked as farmers in the southwestern United States.

8. D Poverty in immigrants' native countries was a push factor; the other choices are pull factors.

9. C Since it describes cramped, unsanitary conditions, this passage is most likely about life in a tenement house.

10. B In crowded tenement houses, poor sanitation often led to outbreaks of disease.

11. A The poor working class most likely lived in tenements in city neighborhoods near factories, railroad yards, and slaughterhouses.

12. B People moved from the farm to the city because of the push factor of the lower need for farm workers; the others are pull factors.

13. D Nativists were native-born American citizens who were fearful of increased immigration.

14. A Immigrants from southern and eastern Europe had religious and cultural traditions that differed from those of many native-born Americans.

15. B The Chinese Exclusion Act of 1882 placed extreme limits on the number of Asians who could enter the United States.

16. D Settlement houses, such as Jane Addams' Hull House, provided numerous services to help immigrants and the urban poor.

17. C Prior to 1915 (1914), war in Europe caused a dramatic drop in immigration from that region.

Lesson 4.1

World War I, p. 41

1. D The value of concern for lives and property after the sinking of the battleship USS *Maine* was the deciding factor in the United States' decision to enter the war.

2. D By the use of the word *however* and by contrasting the congressional resolution with what actually happened, the writer is implying that the United States wanted to expand and to gain territory as a result of the war.

3. C To support its new position in the world, the United States increased the size and strength of its navy.

4. C Because Serbia was closely allied with Russia, when Austria-Hungary declared war on Serbia, Russia and its allies entered the conflict.

5. B This alliance, or group of countries joined together by a common cause, became known as the Central Powers.

6. **B**   Because it offers Mexico support if it declared war on the United States, this passage is most likely taken from the Zimmermann Telegram, which was written by a German foreign minister.

7. **D**   Germany was trying to convince Mexico that it would support Mexico in fighting the United States to reconquer that territory.

8. **D**   Germany's policy of unrestricted submarine warfare, coupled with the release of the Zimmermann Telegram, caused Congress to declare war on Germany.

9. **C**   Germany expected that the United States would join with the Allies.

10. **B**   Until Russia withdrew from the war in 1918, Germany was forced to fight a war on two different fronts.

11. **A**   The initial military focus was towards France.

12. **B**   The Allied Powers occupied most of North Africa, which prevented the Central Powers from moving freely through the area.

13. **A**   Following World War I, Austria-Hungary saw its territory divided into multiple nations, including new nations such as Yugoslavia.

14. **A**   Wilson was a supporter of the League of Nations. Because the address expresses his wish that "the world be made fit and safe to live in," it reflects this support.

15. **C**   Many senators feared that membership in the League of Nations would cause the United States to lose its sovereignty, or ability to act on its own, in case of war.

16. **D**   Wilson outlines safety for "peace-loving" nations who want to decide on "their own institution," a feature of democracy.

17. **A**   The United States was not interested in acquiring new territory.

Lesson 4.2

World War II, p. 45

1. **B**   Referring to the conditions of the Treaty of Versailles as "shackles" is an example of bias because it shows only one side of an issue.

2. **A**   Hitler is referring to the German government that had signed the Treaty of Versailles after World War I.

3. **C**   In 1941, Hitler added the nations of the Balkans to his growing empire.

4. **D**   Since he is referring to a embarking on a "Great Crusade" in 1944, we can conclude that Eisenhower is speaking before D-Day, the invasion of France.

5. **A**   The discovery of Nazi concentration camps, where millions of Jews were murdered, proved that the Allies were not just fighting an enemy, but were eradicating a great evil.

6. **C**   "Home front" refers to the civilian people back in the home country during a war; by saying "home fronts," Eisenhower meant the civilians back home in all the Allied nations.

7. **C**   FDR's list of Japanese actions before using that phrase shows that he wants to describe Japanese aggression.

8. **B**   FDR wanted people to know that Japan had done two things—planned the attack and attacked United States territory.

9. **A**   The United States demanded their unconditional surrender as the only acceptable end to the war with Japan, even at the cost of dropping atomic bombs on their country.

10. **B**   The Holocaust was a result of a specific policy, "the final solution," planned by German leaders and carried out by thousands of people who were part of the genocide.

11. **D** Short-term, the GI Bill helped keep the unemployment rate low by helping returning soldiers enter college rather than the workforce.

Lesson 4.3

The Cold War, p. 49

1. **D** The dashed lines show the military zones created by the Allies during the Yalta Conference.

2. **B** Turkey shared a border with the Soviet Union.

3. **B** After the war, Germany was divided into four zones, each occupied by one of the Allied nations. The zone occupied by the Soviet Union became communist and was ideologically separated from the western areas.

4. **D** The waterways into West Germany from the North Sea were important for shipping goods into West Germany, and having Denmark aligned with the United States and Great Britain meant those lanes would remain open.

5. **A** Berlin was entirely surrounded by East German territory controlled by the Soviets and their East German allies.

6. **C** Winston Churchill gave this border its nickname, the "Iron Curtain."

7. **C** The one area of agreement among the leaders was the creation of the UN to negotiate disputes among nations.

8. **D** The US and the Soviets were rarely in agreement about important international conflicts and issues, and each had a veto in the Security Council.

9. **B** Under a policy of containment, the United States sought to slow the expansion of the Soviet Union's influence, rather than face the Soviet Union in open conflict.

10. **B** If faced with a military force, the Soviet Union would back down, according to Kennan. This is supported by this sentence: " . . . if the adversary has sufficient force and makes clear his readiness to use it, he rarely has to do so."

11. **A** The North Atlantic Treaty Organization was created to stop Soviet expansion in Europe.

12. **D** President Truman then launched the Berlin Airlift. For ten months, American and British planes airlifted millions of tons of supplies to West Berliners.

13. **B** Kennedy sent more troops to West Berlin and called army reserve units to active duty.

14. **C** Following the communist takeover of Cuba in 1959, thousands of refugees fled to the United States.

15. **A** During the Cuban Missile Crisis, President Kennedy set up a naval blockade to prevent Soviet arms from entering Cuba.

16. **C** President Johnson tried to stop the spread of communism in Southeast Asia by sending troops to South Vietnam.

17. **B** France refused to recognize the new communist government based in Hanoi that was led by Ho Chi Minh.

Lesson 4.4

Societal Changes, p. 53

1. **C** According to the speech, the Great Society is "a place where man can renew contact with nature."

2. **B** The Office of Economic Opportunity was established to coordinate poverty programs at the federal level.

3. **A**   According to the speech, the Great Society "demands an end to poverty and racial injustice."

4. **C**   The EEOC, Equal Employment Opportunity Commission, was set up by the Civil Rights Act to investigate charges of discrimination in the workplace.

5. **B**   The Community Action Program gave poor people a greater voice in government decisions affecting their neighborhoods.

6. **A**   President Johnson announced in early 1968 that he would not seek or accept the Democratic Party's nomination for another term as president.

7. **C**   The Nixon Administration's "New Federalism" was designed to return power and tax money to the states.

8. **D**   The Paris Peace Accords ended the Vietnam War. Hostilities would arise again two years later with the defeat of South Vietnam and reunification of Vietnam under communist control.

9. **C**   Nixon felt that the federal government should play a smaller role in the lives of individuals.

10. **D**   The Watergate scandal led to the resignation of Richard Nixon, thus it was the biggest challenge of his presidency.

11. **C**   Only the initial break-in appears to have occurred, as Nixon feels free to turn his attention to other matters instead of defending himself.

12. **D**   Nixon states that United States and Soviet negotiators are meeting to limit nuclear arms and reduce the threat of nuclear war.

13. **B**   This speech attempted to redirect the attention of the nations and the media from the Watergate affair.

14. **D**   China and the Soviet Union had several conflicts, both military and diplomatic, during the Cold War as they fought for worldwide influence.

15. **B**   In 1972, both of these major events occurred.

16. **D**   Nixon hoped he could play the two nations against each other and force the Soviet Union to be less threatening to the United States.

17. **B**   Nixon's visit to China ended 25 years of diplomatic silence between the United States and China.

18. **A**   SALT was an agreement to freeze the production of long-range offensive missiles.

19. **B**   Reforms by Gorbachev that had the goal of greater openness in the Soviet Union led to its eventual dissolution.

Lesson 4.5

Foreign Policy in the 21st Century, p. 57

1. **D**   Osama bin Laden attempted to force Westerners from the Middle East when US troops were stationed in Saudi Arabia.

2. **B**   The bombing of the USS Cole occurred the year before the attacks of the World Trade Center and Pentagon.

3. **D**   Bush states that the attacks were made "because we're the brightest beacon for freedom and opportunity in the world."

4. **C**   Terrorism is a political strategy that uses violence against people or property to achieve a goal.

5. **A**   The al-Qaeda group supports the establishment of theocracies in Islamic nations.

6. **C**   The United States led a coalition force that overthrew the Taliban government in Afghanistan.

7. **D**   President Bush's first response to the attacks of September 11, 2001 was to launch a war against Afghanistan.

8. **C** A fourth plane did not reach its target, but was crashed in rural Pennsylvania following attempts by passengers to overpower the hijackers.

9. **D** This timeline shows how the terrorist attacks affected US foreign policy.

10. **A** Most of the events regarding the US global war on terror have occurred in Iraq and Afghanistan.

11. **D** The Washington Treaty was invoked to set in motion a response to aggression against a NATO member.

12. **B** No weapons of mass destruction were found in Iraq following the United States invasion.

13. **C** Since he identifies hostile actions committed by the Iraqi government, it is most likely that President Bush was arguing in favor of invading Iraq.

14. **B** Sentence 5 uses imagery of mothers and their dead children to evoke an emotional response.

15. **D** Iraq is mentioned most in the speech, and was eventually invaded by a US-led force in 2002.

16. **B** President Bush viewed these nations as an "axis of evil" because each nation was developing weapons of mass destruction that could be used against the United States.

17. **B** Great Britain cooperated with the United States during the invasion of Iraq in 2003.

18. **D** Serious organized fighting was over within a month, but the fighting among insurgent groups and with US troops continued for several years.

Lesson 5.1

Markets, Competition, and Monopolies, p. 61

1. **B** A market is an arrangement or relationship that makes it easier to buy and sell, or exchange goods and services.

2. **A** A market is also a place where goods and services are exchanged. This occurs at a golf course with members paying for the opportunity to play golf or to take golf lessons. Goods and services are not exchanged in a forest preserve, a classroom, or an aircraft carrier.

3. **C** Owners of businesses make goods and services and earn income for them.

4. **B** Price is determined by both how much buyers want an item and how much money the seller is willing to accept in trade, regardless of the costs of production.

5. **D** When resources are scarce or demand for goods and services are high, those without money are at a disadvantage in a market economy.

6. **B** Auto repair shops offer both services (fixing cars) and goods (parts, tires).

7. **D** Economic systems answer three questions: what goods and services to produce, how to produce them, and for whom to produce them.

8. **B** To ensure competition, the government keeps producers from setting prices or limiting supplies.

9. **B** Money or income is what the producers most likely want.

10. **D** Self-interest is the motivation for every transaction, not benevolence.

11. **C** The ad shows services the restaurant provides that sets it apart from the competition.

12. **A** A perfectly competitive market would create the scenario in which the closing of the restaurant would have no effect on the other restaurants' business.

13. **C** In a monopoly, there is only one producer for one type of product.

14. **D** The copyright protects an original work of art, as a patent protects the rights to a new product.

15. D Trust is another term for monopoly.

16. B One of the chief characteristics of a monopoly is that it produces a unique product, one for which there is no easy substitute.

17. A Both laws were intended to prevent new monopolies from forming and break up those that already exist.

18. B The government passes antitrust laws to keep markets competitive and provide freedom of choice for the consumer.

19. B A technological monopoly results when a firm develops a new technology that is used to produce a new product. To protect that product, the firm applies for patents.

20. A A monopoly can set prices for its products without influence from competition.

21. D Products created by monopolies generally cannot be replaced with any similar products.

22. C Pure monopoly only exists in theory.

Lesson 5.2

Factors of Production, p. 65

1. C Scarcity is the combination of a product's having value and its being in shorter supply than the consumer demand for it.

2. B Relative scarcity is a term that is applied to products when there is a large supply of a product, but it is scarce in comparison to the number of people who want it.

3. B The game is no longer in high demand due to overproduction.

4. A Opportunity cost is the value of what was given up in exchange for the choice actually made.

5. A You gave up dinner at the restaurant in exchange for the better phone, so that was what it "cost" you to make that decision.

6. C This choice was based on want, not need.

7. B Business owners can conserve natural resources but cannot control their availability.

8. A Land is nonrenewable because there is a finite amount of it and cannot be developed by humans. Wheat, grain, and trees can be replenished.

9. D Entrepreneurship depends on human creativity.

10. B Nonrenewable resources cannot be easily replenished.

11. B The main factor Samuel Colt changed was how he directed his employees' work processes, making their work more efficient.

12. C By focusing on one or two repeated skills, each worker could perfect and become faster at that skill, and the combined effort would result in a better revolver made in less time.

13. A The improved speed and efficiency would allow the business to make more products with a smaller labor force.

14. A The monotony of one worker performing one task for long periods of time is a drawback of the Colt system from the worker's perspective.

15. C Technology is an aspect of capital resources. It was through technology, especially new tools and methods, that Ford increased productivity.

16. A Goods and services are made by human resources (labor) processing natural resources. For that to occur, capital—technology, tools, and equipment—has to be applied.

17. B   The channel wrapper is a piece of equipment used to produce a good, so it is a capital resource.

18. C   The addition of the channel wrapper reduced the most labor-intensive part of the process of producing candy.

19. D   If the raw materials needed to create a product are unavailable or in short supply, the manufacturer may find a replacement material in order to continue production.

Lesson 5.3

Profits and Productivity, p. 69

1. A   The 1960s showed the least overall fluctuation in housing construction.

2. C   The 1990s was the decade with the strongest growth in housing construction.

3. B   Between 1970 and 1975 marks the highest point on the graph, when companies began building more than 2,400,000 units.

4. A   Housing sales drop during recessions.

5. D   Research, employee training, and new technology all help productivity. Decreasing capital investments would lead to a decrease in productivity.

6. D   The opportunity cost is a temporary production drop while training, purchasing, and research and development take place.

7. A   The training will give company X an advantage after the two months of training have been completed.

8. D   Most of the top firms in the list are pharmaceutical companies.

9. B   Spending money on research and development can make profits for companies.

10. C   Productivity increases when input remains constant, but output increases.

11. C   An increase in capital and resources will boost productivity.

12. A   Property and equipment are part of a company's capital.

13. B   The assembly line made it possible for workers to efficiently perform the same task repeatedly on identical products.

14. D   Because change is discouraged in a traditional economy, people have no incentive to try new ideas or invent new products.

15. D   The United States government cannot take away a citizen's private property without proper compensation.

16. A   In a market economy, human resources, natural resources, and capital resources can be bought and sold, thus increasing their value.

17. C   Workers who receive economic rewards for their labor often work hard to win those incentives, especially if they have been deprived of them previously.

18. D   A performance bonus would be considered an incentive because it would encourage employees to be more productive.

19. D   A traditional economy is no longer in existence on a national level, though it may be found in certain local environments.

Lesson 5.4

Specialization and Comparative Advantage, p. 73

1. D   Today, Americans specialize by working in one type of career field. They do not tan their own leather; they buy it from someone else who does that.

2. **C** A comparative advantage is the ability to produce goods or services at a relatively low opportunity cost compared to other producers.

3. **A** An absolute advantage is the ability to produce more than others using fewer resources.

4. **B** Farmers in Idaho can produce potatoes using fewer resources than farmers in other states.

5. **A** To be efficient, farmers must be able to produce desired results without wasting material, time, or energy.

6. **A** Because Company A can make more mops and brooms than Company B, it has a higher absolute advantage.

7. **C** Those with the lower opportunity cost should specialize in that product or service even if they do not have an absolute advantage.

8. **A** Look at 0 butter on the x-axis and find where the curve intersects the y-axis. This is at 50 guns.

9. **B** About 22—find the 50 butter data point on the x-axis then check the gun data point on the y-axis.

10. **A** The production possibility frontier for gun production is 50.

11. **B** Add the maximum number of guns produced on the y-axis to the maximum amount of butter produced on the x-axis (50 guns + 60 butter).

12. **B** 30 units of butter can be produced when 40 guns are produced.

13. **D** Interdependence happens when producers rely on one another for information, resources, goods, and services.

14. **D** Interdependent businesses share the effects of negative events.

15. **A** Manufacturers depend on retailers to sell their goods, retailers depend on manufacturers to supply them with products to sell, and both depend on shippers to move goods. Answer B is incorrect because competitors are not interdependent. Answer C is incorrect because consumers can function as consumers without relying on other consumers. Answer D is incorrect because, although health care workers and laboratories are interdependent, neither relies on media businesses to carry out their work.

16. **C** Interdependence goes hand in hand with specialization, and therefore raises productivity.

17. **B** The United States *relies* on these imports because it cannot produce enough oil to satisfy demand. Answers A, C, and D are incorrect as they do not relate to a country's reliance on another for a product or service.

18 **D** A strike by rubber industry workers could slow tire production, which the car manufacturer depends on. The situation in Answer A is not a problem as long as the tire supplier can continue to provide the car manufacturer with the tires it needs. The situations in Answers B and C both benefit the car manufacturer by reducing competition.

Lesson 6.1

Microeconomics, p. 77

1. **C** Consumers or buyers influence the demand side of the market.

2. **C** There is government regulation in a mixed economy, but the forces of supply and demand have strong influence in the market

3. **D** A rise in prices is a signal to producers that it is time to increase production. It has a different meaning for consumers. To consumers, it is a signal to buy fewer goods.

4. C A rise in prices is a signal to producers that it is time to increase production. To consumers, it is a signal to buy less of the product.

5. C Microeconomics is the study of individuals and businesses in an economic system. On the other hand, macroeconomics is the study of larger economies. Market equilibrium is the state of a market and supply and demand influence a market; neither, however, is a term describing the study of economics.

6. B The laws of supply and demand drive a market economy.

7. C In a demand curve, there is a negative relationship between price and quantity—as one increases, the other decreases.

8. A Check the Data Table or the Demand Curve table. Look at the y-axis and draw a line to the curve. Then draw a line from that point to the x-axis. This point on the x-axis is the quantity of CDs sold at $15.00.

9. D The quantity of CDs sold when the price changed from $10.00 to $5.00 is three, which is a larger amount than any other price change.

10. B When there is a demand for 5 CDs, the price is $10.

11. D The trend, or direction of change, shown by this graph is that the price of televisions is decreasing over time.

12. C The profit motive means the relationship between the price of a good or service and the quantity supplied is a positive one.

13. B When a product's supply is greater than its demand, its price falls.

14. A High demand can have some harmful consequences, including the creation of a black market for products.

15. C If the price rises, the quantity supplied also rises. Answers A, B, and D do not describe the relationship between price and quantity that applies to supply. If the price drops, the quantity supplied goes down as well.

16. D Both the supply curve and the demand curve are necessary to illustrate market equilibrium.

17. B At 600 million, the supply and demand curves meet. The price at that point is $10.50.

18. C The market reaches the equilibrium point when buyers have no incentive to offer more money for a product, and sellers have no incentive to reduce the price.

Lesson 6.2

Macroeconomics and Government Policy, p. 81

1. A Half of the United States government's revenue comes from income taxes.

2. B Government expenditures are money that is paid out by the government to conduct its business.

3. C When you buy a savings bond, you are loaning the government money to use on projects or services. After a certain amount of time, the government pays off its bonds with interest when they come due. Answers A, B, and D are examples of how the government collects revenue not of how it borrows funds.

4. D The president is addressing the growing federal debt. The president is most likely to address issues of the federal government, not the states. The statement does not address taxes or Social Security.

5. C Federal borrowing is the correct answer. Paying off bonds would reduce debt. Increased taxes and budget surpluses could be used to reduce debt.

6. **B** The highest single category was $1435.2 billion for Medicare and Medicaid.

7. **C** The smallest portion is created by Net Interest.

8. **A** The Defense ($744 billion) is almost equal to the Social Security ($730.1 billion) portion.

9. **B** If the federal deficit were to decrease, the government would pay less in interest because it would not owe as much money.

10. **C** Some tax policies are designed to influence the behavior of individuals or businesses; the other products would be taxed at a high rate to discourage smoking, drinking, and overuse of gasoline.

11. **B** Income taxes were not collected very often during that time.

12. **D** The government uses fiscal policy to stimulate the economy in bad times. Fiscal policy does not affect the supply of money. Fiscal policy does not withhold money from the states, but might result in more money going to the states. While increased spending can increase the debt, that is not the goal.

13. **B** Recent government subsidies have been given to the producers of dairy products, soybeans, wheat, and corn.

14. **B** New regulations can require companies to add steps to their production process, thereby increasing costs.

15. **B** Subsidies are payments to the producer or consumer of a local good or service, which results in lower cost of production and therefore a lower cost for consumers. Answers A and D are the opposite results of a subsidy. Answers C would not be a result of a subsidy.

16. **C** The Federal Reserve works to preserve and maintain the financial stability of the United States.

17. **B** The Federal Reserve has many ways to increase or decrease the supply of money.

18. **C** The Federal Reserve's policies emphasize controlling inflation.

19. **A** One of the main goals of the Federal Trade Commission is to stop unfair business practices.

20. **C** Market failures occur as a result of imperfect competition and gaps between the private coast and the social cost of behaviors or actions.

Lesson 6.3

Macroeconomics, the GDP, and Price Fluctuation, p. 85

1. **B** Gross domestic product (GDP) is determined by multiplying final goods and services by their prices.

2. **B** The amount of goods and services is the most likely reason for a high GDP.

3. **A** GDP includes final goods manufactured within that nation's borders.

4. **A** GDP does not reflect gains made in nonmarket economies, such as barter economies.

5. **D** The GDP of the United States is nearly twice that of China.

6. **C** The United Kingdom's GDP of $2.4 trillion is about twice that of Mexico, which has a GDP of $1.2 trillion.

7. **A** GDP can count negative events as beneficial. Wars and natural disasters can raise GDP, however these events can have an overall negative effect on a nation.

8. **D** Final goods made in the United States and sold in the United States count toward the United States' GDP.

9. **B** Inflation is a rise in the general level of prices over time.

10. **C** Deflation causes the value of the dollar to increase.

11. **C** The same goods will cost $98.00.

12. D The price would rise more than 2 percent because of the cumulative rates over the 10-year-period.

13. C Inflation rose most rapidly between 1973 and 1983.

14. B 1933 saw deflation within the context of the Great Depression.

15. B Unemployment appeared to reach a high of 10 percent at the end of 2009.

16. A The unemployment rose from about 5 percent in 2007 to about 10 percent in 2009.

17. C The unemployment rate counts job seekers who are currently unemployed.

18. A This is the definition of cyclical unemployment.

Lesson 7.1

Major Economic Events, p. 89

1. C When prices increase, people buy less, which shrinks GDP and weakens the economy.

2. B Mass production of the Model T cut its price to 1/3 of the cost before mass production.

3. A A drop in supply when demand is high can lead to price increases.

4. C A boom period is usually reflected in an increase in the GDP.

5. A Rationale: The sell-off in October 1929 was heightened because investors had bought their stocks on margin and would have to find the money to cover the margins if the stocks were sold at a loss.

6. D The Great Depression was so severe that it would have taken a long time for relief programs to help all of those who were poor and homeless.

7. D Building shantytowns on public or unused land would have been more acceptable to the authorities than building them on private land or in the middle of cities.

8. D President Hoover presided over the government as the Great Depression worsened with no relief during the early 1930s.

9. B Roosevelt's New Deal was intended to help stimulate the economy.

10. C Hoover believed that the policies of socialist governments in Europe worsened the Depression there and did not want to repeat that error. Answer A is incorrect because, although Hoover called on state governments to take action, he did not try to coordinate their policies with those of the federal government. Answers B and D are incorrect because Hoover did not act as he did out of concern over his reelection chances or from being distracted.

11. A During the early 1930s, farmers destroyed their crops to reduce the supply, in hopes that increased demand would raise the prices. Answers B and C are incorrect because destroying crops would not create a surplus and increased supply leads to lower, not higher, prices. Answer D is incorrect because destroying crops would not necessarily lower costs.

12. D The Social Security Act provided financial support for people, such as pensions for elderly retired people and people with disabilities.

13. D Though Roosevelt was responding to an immediate need for food and shelter, he also believed that providing people with salaries would help stimulate the economy.

14. C Social Security is a form of relief that provides Americans with a pension in old age.

15. B Roosevelt states that his primary task is to put people to work.

Lesson 7.2

The Relationship Between Politics and Economics, p. 93

1. **C** The speech indicates that Coolidge believed individual prosperity was possible only with limited taxes.

2. **B** Coolidge implies that it is unjust to tax rich people at a higher rate, and that they should not be punished for their prosperity. This indicates that Coolidge does not believe that the system helped certain people to become rich but that they earned it themselves.

3. **C** Coolidge rejects the idea that the rich should be taxed more and makes the point that those who are successful should not be punished for their success.

4. **C** The New Deal used Keynesian economic ideas to intervene in the economy during the Great Depression.

5. **B** The country was producing more goods than Americans could buy, which led to hard economic times. Answers A, C, and D are other factors that may have influenced imperialism, but are not the reasons that the United States needed to find new markets for their goods.

6. **C** The destruction and instability caused by war can disrupt business and everyday life.

7. **A** As the value of a country's currency falls, imports will become relatively less expensive, not less so. It may gain export jobs, but not because of the price of labor. Prices will not go down, but producers might raise them to meet profit goals, since the currency is worth less.

8. **B** Market economies tend to be efficient, produce ample quantities of consumer foods, and have high per capita GDP. The correct answer is B because of the tendency of these economies to have periods of decline alternating with periods of growth.

9. **C** An open-door policy gave all countries equal trading rights with China.

10. **B** Annexation is taking control of another country or territory, as the United States did with Hawaii in 1898.

11. **A** She states that the will of God made her heir apparent and the grace of God made her queen.

12. **B** The queen considers Hawaii to be an independent nation whose rule should be in the hands of chiefs.

13. **B** An increase in unemployment due to disruptions in businesses could cause homelessness.

14. **C** War and political instability frighten away investors.

15. **B** Humanitarian aid improves people's lives and reduces suffering.

16. **C** Financial aid can provide economic stability, which can lead to political stability, which is in the best interest of United States foreign policy.

Lesson 7.3

The Scientific and Industrial Revolutions, p. 97

1. **B** The scientific method is the process used by scientists for testing ideas through experimentation and careful observation.

2. **D** The Scientific Revolution was an era in which many discoveries and many new ideas came about in a short period of time.

3. **B** The caravel and carrack are ships. The quadrant is a device sailors used to calculate their location on the sea. Sailors used a compass to navigate because it indicates magnetic north and they could determine in what direction they were sailing.

4. **D** Antonie von Leeuwenhoek discovered cells in living matter through observation with a microscope.

5. **B** Scientists use the scientific method to try to explain the facts they have observed by testing theories about those facts.

6. **B** The astrolabe allowed sailors to use the position of the sun and stars to determine the time of a celestial event, such as a sunrise or sunset.

7. **C** The astrolabe helped make European exploration possible.

8. **B** An industrial revolution shifts the economy from farming and trading to the manufacturing of goods.

9. **B** Machines powered by water and steam needed to be housed in factories, rather than private homes or workshops. Answers A and D are incorrect because people were needed to run the machines and sometimes children were used in factory work. Answer C is incorrect because government policy was not the cause for this shift.

10. **C** As part of Britain's colonial empire, India sent tons of raw cotton to be used in England's cloth-making mills. Answers A, B, and D are incorrect because Britain had those resources.

11. **A** Coal was the natural resource used to run the newly invented steam engine and allowed Great Britain to become an industrial society. Answers B, C, and D are other factors of production that enabled Britain to become an industrial society but were not related to the steam engine.

12. **A** According to the table, cotton mills were concentrated in northwest England, so movement into cities was highest in that area of England.

13. **D** In the first half of the 19th century, the development of railroads helped speed the development of the Industrial Revolution in England.

14. **D** Great Britain needed the raw materials supplied by its colonies to help create its industrial society.

15. **C** The cotton gin had an impact on the South, but not the interior of the country. The slave codes were not an invention. The locomotive made transportation of goods and people to the interior faster.

16. **B** Industrialization affected farming as new machines replaced farm workers.

17. **A** Between 1800 and 1850, the cities grew rapidly as people moved to the cities to be close to factories and mills where they worked.

18. **C** Before labor unions, employers were free to treat workers according to their own company's rules.

19. **D** Only the youngest and smallest children would likely be able to fit under running machines.

20. **A** Poverty most likely forced families to send their children to work in factories.

Lesson 8.1

Savings and Banking, p. 101

1. **B** Banks never send cash through the mail.

2. **D** The three main services provided by banks are to keep money safe, provide a way to transfer funds, and loan money.

3. **A** Banks keep reserves of cash available to cover depositors' withdrawals.

4. **C** This is an example of transferring money.

5. **A** Banks advertise that they have insurance to honor their promises to return deposits, if necessary

6. **D** The cash reserves will be kept for future use.

7. **D** The first credit unions provided emergency loans to their members.

8. **A** In the past, different banks offered different types of services, but now most offer the same services.

9. **B** Bank deposits are insured.

10. **A** Banks profit from the fees and interest earned when they loan money.

11. **D** These institutions provided services to ordinary people.

12. **C** Their customers were those not served by commercial banks.

13. **D** Having a personal checking account allows you to withdraw money, use an ATM, pay bills electronically, use an ETF, and write checks.

14. **C** Both the bank and the institution that received the check may charge a fee if you write a check for an amount greater than the account's balance.

15. **B** All banks are required to protect the privacy of their depositors.

16. **C** Banks typically charge a penalty fee for overdrafts.

17. **C** She is writing the check to Leadville Water Company.

18. **D** In order to be cashed or deposited, a check must be endorsed, or signed, by the check's recipient, the person to whom it is issued.

19. **C** It means the bank must pay the check immediately, either through cash in the form of currency or through an electronic transfer of funds.

20. **B** The number in the bottom left of a check indicates which bank issued that check.

Lesson 8.2

Types of Consumer Credit, p. 105

1. **B** If borrower defaults on a secured loan, the lender assumes the asset or property that secured the loan.

2. **A** Interest and fees provide profits for credit card companies.

3. **C** Credit reports indicate if a person's identity has been stolen or used to purchase items illegally.

4. **B** Interest on home equity loans is usually tax deductible.

5. **B** A credit score reflects how well someone pays his or her bills.

6. **D** Falling behind on loan or credit card payments can reduce a person's credit score.

7. **A** A drop in a person's credit score usually results in a more difficult time getting credit.

8. **D** Credit agencies get their information from banks and credit card companies.

9. **C** Home equity loans typically have low interest rates, and the interest can often be deducted from taxes.

10. **A** Legally, you are allowed to obtain your credit report once each year for free from a reputable consumer credit reporting agency.

11. **C** Because a car is a large purchase and would have to be paid off over a period of time, buying a car on a credit card is not advisable because the interest rates are usually higher than those of other types of credit.

12. **D** High interest, declining property values, and an unreliable source of income should all be red flags to home buyers.

13. **B** The finance charge is the amount you pay for credit.

14. **C** Secured loans are used for these types of purchases.

15. **B** Interest is not charged on balances completely paid off each month.

16. **A** This information must be disclosed by lenders before issuing credit.

17. D APRs vary by lender.

18. A According to the information in the passage, credit card debt is becoming more of a problem with each passing generation.

19. D This trend shows that credit card companies see a good potential market in younger customers.

20. C Most credit card debt accrued by young people is not necessarily spent on wants, but rather also on essentials, leading to the conclusion that costs have increased.

21. C This amount is an increase of the same amount during the previous generation.

Lesson 8.3

Consumer Credit Laws, p. 109

1. A The Fair Credit Reporting Act states that consumers have a right to have access to their credit reports.

2. C By having only five or fewer numbers from the credit card appear on a receipt, consumers are protected from unauthorized people using their credit card.

3. C The Truth in Lending Act limits a consumer's liability.

4. D The Equal Credit Opportunity Act prohibits discrimination in credit transactions on the basis of certain personal characteristics.

5. B The Consumer Credit Protection Act is an "umbrella" act that includes acts related to consumer credit protection.

6. C The writer is questioning the effectiveness of the Credit CARD Act.

7. A The writer believes that federal credit card protection has been inadequate to deal with the problems facing cardholders.

8. B Credit card providers had to provide consumers with information about the card's annual percentage rate (APR) and annual fees.

9. B The APR is the most significant feature to compare credit card offers.

10. D Most companies offer low credit limits to first-timers because they do not want to take high risks.

11. B No-interest loans are a prohibited incentive.

12. B The CFPB is concerned with laws and regulations related to the sale of financial products and services.

13. A The previous focus of government agencies regarding the financial marketplace was the protection of banks and the development of monetary policy.

14. C Each month the credit card provider would add interest to the balance, making the time period for paying off the balance last longer.

15. A Paying the balance due is the only way to avoid interest charges that are shown in the estimated payment column on the right.

16. D The financial crisis of 2007 led to the creation of the Consumer Financial Protection Bureau through the Dodd-Frank Wall Street Reform and Consumer Protection Act.

17. B Because federal law requires credit card providers to be consistent in payment dates and times, this consumer's next due date will most likely be 5/20/12.

Lesson 9.1

Development of Ancient Civilizations, p. 113

1. **B** The Nile's annual floodwaters made agriculture possible, and this in turn gave rise to Egyptian civilization.

2. **C** Most ancient civilizations developed near sources of water, such as rivers.

3. **A** The delta is where the Nile empties into the Mediterranean Sea.

4. **D** These pyramids and temples reflect the ancient Egyptians' religious belief in an afterlife.

5. **D** Civilization developed along the Tigris and Euphrates Rivers in present-day Iraq.

6. **C** The pharaoh Khufu was buried in the Great Pyramid of Giza.

7. **C** The economies of ancient Egypt and the Indus River Valley were dependent on agriculture.

8. **A** The pharaoh represented the god Ra.

9. **C** The Aryans introduced the caste system, which divided society into four social classes.

10. **D** The Egyptian and Indian subcontinent civilizations were centered near rivers.

11. **A** The Aryan social system divided people into categories called castes.

12. **D** The language of Harappa and Mohenjo-Daro has never been deciphered.

13. **B** A mandate is another word for "command."

14. **A** Because the Mandate of Heaven holds that the right to rule depends on virtue, we can conclude that those who opposed the Shang dynasty believed that its rulers were not virtuous.

15. **B** The Mandate of Heaven gave Chinese dynasties divine command, and the embodiment of the Egypt ruler as the sun god gave the ruler the power of the divine.

16. **D** The Huang He regularly flooded, causing widespread loss of life.

17. **A** The religion of the Shang people included ancestor worship.

18. **C** The geography of Greece isolated groups of people, giving rise to independent city-states.

19. **C** Greek city-states were established with a hill at the center of each.

20. **C** Athens was the city-state that pioneered the system of democracy.

21. **A** In Rome, all male citizens were members of the Assembly of the People, which made laws, and in Athens, all male citizens could vote.

22. **B** In a republic such as that of ancient Rome, elected representatives govern.

23. **C** Ancient Greece and Rome were unique in the level to which their citizens participated in governing.

Lesson 9.2

Nationhood and Statehood, p. 117

1. **B** The Mediterranean Sea and the Red Sea are physical boundaries because they are natural features that separate two regions from one another.

2. **A** Lake Victoria makes up over half of the border between Uganda and Tanzania.

3. **C** The Rio Grande is a physical boundary because it forms a natural border between Texas and Mexico.

4. **C** The Pacific Ocean serves as a border for Hawaii, Alaska, Washington, Oregon, and California.

5. **B** The borders of ten states occur at the Mississippi River.

6. **B** 30° north passes through the United States and Mexico.

7. **A** The border between the United States and Mexico is partially geometric (political) and partially geographic (the Rio Grande).

8. **A** The border between Alaska and Canada follows a line of longitude.

9. **C** Lines of latitude increase in value with greater distance from the equator, either north or south.

10. **B** The Soviet Union was created in 1922, and its borders changed when it was dissolved in 1991.

11. **A** The creation of new borders signified that Kazakhstan had become an independent nation.

12. **D** Borders were roughly the same as the nations reemerged after decades of Soviet domination.

13. **C** The border between Russia and Mongolia did not change after the dissolution of the Soviet Union.

Lesson 9.3

Human Activity and the Environment, p. 121

1. **C** The president wants to develop renewable sources of energy, such as wind and solar energy.

2. **A** The United States needs new sources of energy to meet the demands of its growing population.

3. **B** Sustainable development encourages the use of renewable energy sources.

4. **A** Coal and gas are nonrenewable fossil fuels.

5. **C** Because industries were less active following World War II, there were fewer greenhouse gas emissions, which led to lower temperatures.

6. **B** Because greenhouse gas emissions increase when the economy improves, it can be inferred that trying to curb greenhouse gas emissions would harm the economy.

7. **A** Droughts and floods change how much water is available to a community at any given time.

8. **C** Natural gas, coal, and oil result from decaying carbon matter, usually under pressure.

9. **D** The greenhouse effect has been the most serious incentive for sustainable development.

10. **C** Sustainable development advocates urge people to reduce consumption of natural resources, like oil and gas.

11. **B** Higher standards of living are creating an increased demand for resources

12. **A** China is currently the world's top producer of greenhouse gases and also has the world's highest population.

13. **C** Consumer demand plays the largest role in influencing the production of goods.

14. **D** Warmer temperatures create higher ocean levels due to melted ice in polar regions.

15. **D** Sustainable development focuses on reusing and recycling resources as well as reducing their use.

16. **B** In eight of the ten years shown here, recycling made up the largest portion of tire use.

17. **A** 2011 has the lowest amount of tires going into landfills, which means it had the highest percentage of tires being reused, recycled, or used as fuel.

18. **A** Concerns about the safety of reused tires may lead to a lower number of tires designated for that purpose.

Lesson 10.1

Concepts of Region and Place, p. 125

1. **A** All living organisms on Earth live on the layer known as the crust.

2. **C** The outer core is made of liquid metal, and the inner core is made of solid metal.

3. **A** Earth's thickest layer, its mantle, is made of solid rock.

4. **B** All countries combined produce about 15,000 metric tons, so Chile produces about one-third of the world's copper.

5. **C** North and South America have three countries that are among the world's leading producers.

6. **C** An isthmus is a narrow strip of land that connects two large land masses, for example, the isthmus of Panama.

7. **A** There may be several different cultures in one country.

8. **D** Because of the lack of sunlight and low oxygen levels, ocean depths would contain the smallest populations and lowest diversity of marine ecosystems.

9. **A** These are features of a grassland ecosystem.

10. **D** Both of these ecosystems feature year-round low temperatures.

11. **B** Biomes are regions that contain many similar ecosystems.

12. **C** Antarctica has only one ecosystem and biome.

13. **B** All biomes are either terrestrial or aquatic.

14. **B** Areas closest to the Equator have a more tropical climate than those farthest from it.

15. **B** The cities are all located on the coast in temperate or subtropical climates, ensuring that the temperatures are moderate in both summer and winter.

16. **A** The desert is less than half the size of Australia.

17. **A** Weipa's location guarantees it more rainfall than most parts of Australia.

Lesson 10.2

Natural and Cultural Diversity, p. 129

1. **D** Australia is smaller than Antarctica and Europe, the next biggest contenders.

2. **C** All five bodies make up a continuous global ocean.

3. **C** Surrounded by mountains, the interior of Australia would be blocked from receiving any significant rainfall.

4. **B** The Arctic Circle has a cold, dry climate, which leads to a low density of plant and animal life.

5. **D** Diversity is defined as variety.

6. **C** Higher temperatures and rainfall contribute together to biodiversity.

7. **C** These are all elements of culture.

8. **B** Multicultural countries contain many different cultures.

9. **D** The distinctive culture of Japan includes its language, which is spoken by most people living in Japan.

10. **A** These languages have a common ancestor, Indo-European.

11. D Large numbers of Germans, English, Africans, and Irish migrated to America between 1607 and 1820.

12. B If you have a diverse ancestry, you cannot accurately report it to the Census Bureau.

13. B Bison are grazing animals, and as the Great Plains is grassland, the Lakota would have included bison in their diet.

14. B Urban sprawl is a term for the expansion of a population beyond city limits to outlying areas.

15. A Lakes and oceans provide transportation, fishing, and tourism.

16. B The northwest quadrant of the United States contains the most states with very low population concentration.

Lesson 10.3

Population Trends and Issues, p. 133

1. D Nevada, Arizona, and Colorado all surpassed 30 percent growth, so there is probably a need for increased government services in the southwest.

2. A Pennsylvania saw the lowest rate of population growth among these four states.

3. D Generally a high fertility rate and low mortality rate means a growing population.

4. C The government uses census data in part to determine where new government services might be needed.

5. B The map shows Japanese migration from East Asia to North America and South America.

6. A Many Europeans settled across the United States.

7. B Europeans could migrate into Asia by land rather than over water.

8. A Buffalo presents an example of urban sprawl because its urban areas have spread into the outlying areas.

9. C These are part of the Buffalo Metropolitan Area.

10. D The map shows that East Aurora is part of the urbanized Buffalo Metropolitan Area that is characterized by sprawl—a spread of urban areas into outlying regions.

11. A The Canadian border and Lake Erie prohibit uniform growth.

12. D 1980–2010 is the period in which residential areas and businesses moved into outlying areas.

13. D Cultural diffusion refers to the spreading of cultural traits to other areas that happens when people migrate.

14. D A high infant mortality rate suggests the need for improved prenatal and postnatal care and perhaps problems with child nutrition. Answers A and B are incorrect because these statistics have to do with population growth. Answer C is incorrect because the data would include causes of death that were not related to health care and address the population as a whole rather than only children.

15. A The lesson uses this example, as well as people fleeing Germany during World War II, and Rwanda and Burundi in the 1990s to escape civil war, to illustrate how involuntary migrations cause people to become displaced, or forced to move due to conflict. Such people are considered refugees because they do not voluntarily leave their homes. Answer B is incorrect because it describes migration for economic reasons. Answer C is incorrect because it describes internal rather than international migration. Answer D is incorrect because, although it describes forced movement, those forced into slavery were not refugees.

16. B If the economic performance of a country is improving, then its standard of living is improving. Make sure students understand that these two generally go hand in hand